MANAGEMENT OF NEW ISSUE SERVICES

(A Study of Lead Merchant Bankers)

MANAGEMENT OF NEW ISSUE SERVICES

(A Study of Lead Merchant Bankers)

By

Dr. P.M. Meera Mohiadeen

M.Com., B.Ed., M.Phil., Ph.D.,

Reader in Commerce

Jamal Mohamed College

Tiruchirapalli–620 020

DISCOVERY PUBLISHING HOUSE

NEW DELHI-110002

First Published-2003

ISBN 81-7141-723-X

Published by

DISCOVERY PUBLISHING HOUSE
4831/24, Ansari Road, Prahlad Street,
Darya Ganj, New Delhi-110002 (India)
Phone: 23279245 • Fax: 91-11-23253475
E-mail:dphtemp@indiatimes.com

Printed at:

Tarun Offset Printers, Delhi-53

Dedicated

To

My Father

(LATE) M.K. PITCHAI MOHIADEEN

and my Wife

(LATE) NAHIDHA (ALIAS) M.S. UMMA SALMA

Preface

The process of Liberalisation, Globalisation and Privatisation have encouraged a large number of companies to raise finance through the public issues, which in most of the cases are being oversubscribed many times. This phenomenon has resulted in increasing a number of equity investors in this country. For instance the SEBI report stated that there were 30.8 million mutual fund investors as on 31st March, 2002. Further, there has been a phenomenal increase in the institutions, which provide new issue management and other allied services to the investors and the issuers to the public issue. Next, there has been awakening amongst the masses, particularly the middle class and salaried group to invest their savings in the securities market to have a better and quick appreciation in its value. The formation of a separate body namely Securities and Exchange Board of India (SEBI) to regulate and control, both the security market and the intermediaries like the brokers, underwriters, registrar to issue, bankers to the issue, financial advertising agencies and lead merchant bankers have necessitated to study the new issue management services. Further, the development of depository system, on-line trading and global equity market all have pave the way to trigger the scope and functioning of the new issue management services. On account of increasing importance of the subject of New Issue Management Services and Financial Services, it has now been included as a special subject in all Commerce and Management Sources conducted by different Indian Universities and professional bodies. Thus the scope of new issue management and merchant banking in our country has widened manifold.

Keeping in view the requirements of Lead Merchant Bankers, Banks, Financial Institutions, Project and Financial

Consultants, Promoters, Managers, Underwriters, Brokers, Registrars to the Issue, and investors in shares and debentures and public depositors the present volume focused on the new issue management services of 26 sample lead merchant bankers in India. Firstly, the study described merchant banker's organisational structure and general profile. Secondly, it assessed the functioning of the merchant bankers in the pre-issue and post-issue management phases and evaluated the new issue performance. Thirdly, it also studied the impact of the SEBI's measures towards new issue management regulations. Finally, it concluded that merchant banking business has experienced active new issue business. I hope this book will serve the purpose of all concerned. I hope that both the students and teachers will find the book useful and rewarding. Constructive suggestions for improvement in the book will be gratefully acknowledged.

Dr. P.M. Meera Mohiadeen

Acknowledgement

I own my deep sense of gratitude to almighty for having graced me to do the work. I gratefully record my deep indebtness to my wife (Late) M.S. Umma Salma alias Nahidha for having provided me constant encouragement, moral support and conducive environment in the family for conducting the research work when she was living with me. But for her help, this study would not have been completed; it my duty to pray God to rest her soul in peace.

I gratefully record my indebtness to my Guide and Supervisor Dr. N. Shaik Mohamed, M.Com., M.Phil., Ph.D., Reader in Commerce, Jamal Mohamed College, Tiruchirapalli for having given me an untiring and judicious guidance and inspiring encouragement in the research work. He has enriched me at every stage of my research work in the form of constructive criticism, suggestions, comments and extended valuable guidance. But for his able and expert guidance, this study would not have been completed. It is my duty to express my profound sense of gratitude and sincere thanks to him.

Words and inadequate to express my hearty thanks to the entire sampled merchant banking organisations for enabling me to do the research work in this regard. My special thanks in this regard to Mr. Kotta Raju, Assistant Manager, Merchant banking division, State Bank of Hyderabad.

In my field study, a host of merchant banking officers had been of immense help to me from time to time in the collection of primary data. Mr. Muralidharan, Assistant Manager, Springfield Financial Services, Hyderabad, S. Prabhkaran,

Senior Project Executive, Indbank Merchant Banking Services, Chennai, Mr. Vasudevan, Vijay Growth Financial Services Ltd., Hyderabad, Mr. Naresh Kumar, Vikaspuri, New Delhi, deserve mention in this regard.

I express my special thanks to Mr. R.K. Perumal, F.C.A. Chartered Accountant, Kaliaperumal R and Associates, Hyderabad and Tiruchirapalli for his immense help in getting permission from the private sector merchant bankers in Hyderabad and Chennai to do research in Merchant Banking. I also express my sense of gratitude to Mr. Paresh, Madras Stock Exchange in Chennai.

I am thankful to Chief Librarians H.T. Parkh Library, Institute of Financial Management and Research, Chennai, Ratan Tata Library, New Delhi and Indian Council of Social Science Research, New Delhi. I sincerely thank Dr. A.M. Mohamed Sindhasha, Reader in Commerce, Jamal Mohamed College, Tiruchirapalli, for the encouragement and timely help. He has enriched me at every stage of my research work in the form of constructive criticism, suggestions, comments and extended valuable guidance.

I express my sincere thanks to Mr. V. Muruganantham, Accountants Officer, Sri Aravind Industries Private Limited, Tiruchirapalli for his immense help in collection of secondary data.

I am very much thankful to Proprietor, Discovery Publishing House in New Delhi, who has made strenuous efforts in making this book to see the light of the day within short term.

Dr. P.M. Meera Mohiadeen

Contents

Abbreviations

AFI : All India Financial Institution

AIPMA : All India Private Merchant Bankers Association

AMBI : Association of Merchant Bankers of India

CCI : Controller of Capital Issues

EPS : Earnings Per Share

AIFIs : All India Financial Institutions

BSE : Bombay Stock Exchange

CMIE : The Centre for Monitoring of Indian Economy

FIs : Financial Institutions

FII : Foreign Institutional Investors

ICICI : Industrial Credit and Investment Corporation of India

IDBI : Industrial Development Bank of India

IFCI : Industrial Finance Corporate of India

IPO : Initial Public Offering

LIC : Life Insurance Corporation of India

LMBs : Lead Merchant Bankers

MB : Merchant Banking

MBs : Merchant Bankers

NA : Not Available

NB : Nationalised Bank

NBS : Nationalised Bank Subsidiary

NBFCs : Non Banking Financial Companies

NIM	:	New Issue Market
NRIs	:	Non Resident Indians
NSE	:	National Stock Exchange of India Limited
OTCEI	:	Over the Counter Exchange of India
PSUs	:	Public Sector Undertaking
PSB	:	Private Sector Bank
PMB	:	Private Merchant Banker
RBI	:	Reserve Bank of India
SEBI	:	The Securities and Exchange Board of India
SEs	:	Stock Exchanges
SFI	:	State Financial Institution
UTI	:	Unit Trust of India

1

Design and Execution of the Study

PRELUDE

Definition of New Issue

Financial markets comprise of capital market which deals with long term funds and money market with short term funds. The capital market has two important segments namely New Issue Market/Primary market and Secondary market/stock market. "New Issues" constitute a term applied to offers to the general public of stock or shares in companies already existing, or new companies being formed, also offers by municipalities, governments etc."[1]

New Issue Market

New Issues Market deals with the raising of fresh capital either for cash or for consideration other than cash by companies and encompasses all institutions dealing in issues. The forms of these issues include equity shares, preference shares, debentures, bonds, deposits, miscellaneous loans etc. These new issues are typically broken into two groups: 1. Seasoned new issues and 2. Initial Public Offerings (IPOs). Seasoned new issues are issued by companies with existing public markets for their securities. The IPOs are issued by new companies/closely held companies without public market for their securities for the purpose of new projects, expansion, modernisation, diversification of the existing projects etc. Therefore, the new issues mean releasing the corporate securities to the investors by an existing company or a new company. In the Secondary market or stock market, the existing securities are bought and sold.

Methods of Flotation

There are different methods adopted for flotation of new issues. They are:

1. **Offer through Prospectus of Public Issue.** Involves inviting subscription from the public through issue of a prospectus.
2. **Offer for Sale.** Under this method, the company sells all shares at an agreed price to brokers who in turn resale them to the investing public.
3. **Private Placement.** It involves selling of securities privately by the issuing company or broker to the selected investors.
4. **Right Issue.** It is the method of raising additional finance from existing members by offering securities to them on a pre-emptive basis.
5. **Bonus Issue.** Bonus shares are issued to existing shareholders of the company by capitalising the free reserves and profit of the company.

Influence on Savings and Investment in Capital Market

"The tone of the capital market depends on the savings and investment in the economy and the performance of the industry and the economy in general."[2] The supply of the capital is dependent upon the rate of the savings in economy. Savings emanate from three sources: (1) Household sector, (2) Private corporate sector, and (3) Public sector. The financial intermediaries are mainly engaged in mobilising personal savings. The savings of corporate bodies arise from the undistributed profits which are normally taken to reserves.

Government surplus arises from the budget surplus on current account. The savings constitute the aggregate pool of the national savings. The pattern of the gross savings and investment over the plan periods are presented in the Annexure I. Gross Domestic Savings during the first plan period was 10.4 per cent on GDP and it was stepped up to 22.4 per cent on GDP during the seventh plan period.

Among the three sources, Household constitutes the primary source for capital formation in the country. Their direct subscription to new issues and investment in different schemes of mutual funds are the sources of funds for the primary market. The proportion of shares and debentures in the total gross financial savings of the household sector has increased significantly from 3.4 per cent in 1980–81 to 10.3 per cent in 1993–94; if we add units, the increase is seen to be much larger i.e. from 3.7 per cent to 16.3 per cent during the same period. These details are presented in the Annexure II.

"It reflects a major shift in the financial savings pattern of the household sector from the bank deposits to the share and debentures of corporate sector and unit of mutual funds and UTI."[3] According to RBI estimates, "during 1996–97, 10.6 per cent of household savings went into financial assets compared to 8.4 per cent in the previous year".[4]

Corporate Sector Performance in New Issue Market

The corporate performance is another major indicator which attracts the investors to the new issue market. Some evidence of encouraging performance of Indian Corporate sector (1983–84 to 1989–90) is shown in the Annexure III. Further, the "Industrial production in 1994–95 is believed to have risen by 8.3 per cent (April-Dec. 1994) as against 4.7 per cent in 1993–94 (April-March) The highest increase has been in capital goods—22.2 per cent against a decline of 5.1 per cent in the previous year".[5] It is evident from Annexure III that the equity issues were constantly favoured by Indian Public Limited Companies during 1983–84 and 1989–90.

The new issues have increased from a meagre Rs. 25 crore in 1957 to Rs. 58 crore in 1975 to Rs. 26,456 crore in 1994–95 (see Annexure IV). The annual average of new issues has increased from Rs. 17 crore during 1951–55 to Rs. 12,349 crore during 1991–94. Thus "an accelerating or exponential increase in new issues has occurred during the 80's and 90's.[6] Even though, the new issues market is organisationally distinct from the secondary market, it is closely associated with secondary market. Because, "rise in the prices of established securities resulting from stock market boom, history shows, has created upsurge in new issue activity".[7] Therefore, the state of secondary market, influences the new issue market. The growth of capital market over the years are presented in the Annexure V.

New Issue Management Services

New issue management services usually entail the management of new issues on behalf of a corporate clients or institutions, the origination, underwriting and distribution and all other administrative work in connection with the new issues. It involves varied functions. It starts with designing the capital structure, type of issue instrument, preparing draft prospectus, complying the various legal requirements, finalising the marketing strategy and end with the mobilisation of funds from the investors. To perform the above functions there should be some specialised skills needed. The company promoter can not perform the new issue management function individually and make the issue a success. The promoter must depend on so many new issue management agencies like merchant-bankers, underwriter, share broker, issue houses, print media. In new issue markets, a merchant-banker is one of the many important agencies retained by the company to assist in mobilisation of funds. However, there is a critical difference between the merchant-banker and other agencies, he selects and co-ordinates the other agencies. In the new issue process, merchant-banker has to shoulder a major responsibility and is indirectly responsible for the acts of other agencies. Therefore, it is essential to understand the significance of merchant banking in new issue management services.

Definition of Merchant-banker

The merchant-banker is one who is arranging or mobilising or assisting investible funds from investors through stock/bonds/preference shares on behalf of the issuer, for corporate establishment or for expansion and diversification purpose of the corporate bodies. The merchant-banker is a conduit between the issuer and investors. He is like a water diviner, to locate the latent financial resources beneath the chest of the investors and pump out the funds from them and channelling into the corporate sector needs. As per SEBI (Merchant-bankers) rules, "merchant-banker" means any person who is engaged in the business of issue management either by making arrangements regarding selling, buying or subscribing to securities as manager, consultant, advisor or rendering corporate advisory service in relation to such issue management.

Growth of Merchant Banking

Merchant banking activity was formally initiated into the Indian capital markets scenario when National and Grindlays Bank (NGB) obtained the license from RBI in 1967. Following Grindlays Bank, the first National City Bank (FNCB) has set up its merchant banking division in 1970. Consequent to the recommendations of the banking commission in 1972, the State Bank of India started the merchant banking division in 1972. The real thrust in the new issue market was provided by the enactment of the Foreign Exchange Revolution Act (FERA) in 1973 and subsequent directives from government to dilute the holdings of foreign companies at attractive prices. As a result, foreign companies' public issues gave investors an instant appreciation and gave a lot of scope to the merchant-banker to do the issue management activities. Therefore, "the concept of 'Issue Management' started getting popularity and, as a natural consequences thereof, the major banks operating began expanding their activities in this innovative arena".[8]

Before that, there were enough evidences of new issue activity in India. The managing agency houses, stock brokers, investment companies, commercial banks and developmental financial institutions had been rendering the merchant banking services in one form or another.

Following the issue of notification under Section 6(1)(o) of the Banking Regulation Act during 1984, commercial banks were permitted to set up subsidiaries with not less than 51 per cent of share-holding for under-writing equipment leasing business or invest share within the limits specified in section 19(2) of the above Act. This modification provided the real thrust to the banks, especially among the early initiators, and a number of subsidiaries were established to undertake merchant banking, leasing and mutual fund activities. "The booming stock market in the 1980's saw many a merchant-banker to set up shop. Institutions, banks and brokers entered the merchant banking".[9]

The mid of 1980's late Mr. Rajiv Gandhi, then Prime Minister, initiated the era of liberalisation in the financial sector and the Indian capital markets first came into the focus of government attention in 1987. The government of India on April 12, 1988 constituted the Securities and Exchange Board of India, with a view to promoting orderly and healthy development of securities market in providing adequate protection to investors. Subsequently, the government of India repealed the Capital Issues (Control) Act, 1947 and promulgated "the Securities and Exchange Board of India Act, 1992". Under the SEBI regime, the companies are free to fix up the price on their own. Therefore, the development and growth of merchant banking in India has taken place only after the banking commission recommendation in the year 1972, the financial sector reforms and the formation of the SEBI has a separate body in 1992.

The consents and acknowledgement granted by the erstwhile Controller of Capital Issue and the present SEBI for capital issue and bonus issue are given in Annexure VI. It is evident from the Annexure VI that during 1984–95 period the grant of consents/acknowledgements/clearance by the CCI, companies to issue shares and debentures has increased significantly. It was Rs. 1787.4 crore during 1984–85 but in the recent years it has gone up to Rs. 17121.0 crore which has risen 9 times.

Impact of New Issues Market on Merchant Banking

The upsurge and down slide in the new issue market has its direct impact on the merchant banking segment. For instance, in 1989–90 there were 78 merchant-bankers. They handled 187 issues and helped companies raise 2793 crore through equity issues. But in 1994–95 103 merchant-bankers, out of the total of 816 merchant-bankers in operation, handled a record 1343 public issues raising RS. 13, 311 crore.[10]

Therefore, the new issue market has witnessed an exploding growth from 187 new issues during 1989–90 to a whopping 1343 issue during 1994–95. At the same time, the total number of merchant-bankers involved in the handling of the issues also went up from 78 to 816. During the recent past, the new issue market has been in the doldrums and the number of issue as well as the amount raised from the new issue market have been substantially reduced. The number of merchant-bankers has drastically been reduced. For instance, the number of merchant-bankers registered with the SEBI has been coming down from a high of 1163 in 1996–97 to less than 300 at the end of 1997–98.[11]

During the period 1996–97 the number of public issue was 753 and amount raised was Rs. 11,648 crore. Up to October 1997, the number of issues was 62 and amount raised was Rs. 2861.94 crore. These details are presented in the Annexure VII. This causes concern not only to the merchant-bankers but also to the issuers, investing public and to the Government too. The development of merchant banking from 1967 to 1997 is presented in the Annexure VIII.

Statement of the Problem

Merchant banking is a vital segment of the economy. In our country, there are hundreds of merchant-bankers rendering their service to the investors. Though we have quantitative growth of the merchant-bankers, the qualitative growth is not good. There are multiple reasons for the poor performance of the merchant bankers.

One of the reasons for such poor performance is the improper price fixed up by the merchant-bankers for the new issues. The improper price may be due to manipulation done by the issuer company and others. This results in failure of many new issues. Another reason for the poor performance of the merchant-bankers is the mutual understanding between the issuer companies and merchant-bankers. It is said that such type of close relationship may result in bogus issues. This is not only a loss to the issuing companies but also to investors at large and the economy too. This is evident from the Ministry of Finance's independent study. The study is based on primary shares issues made by 2012 companies between April 1994 and March 1996, of which 1450 companies are trading below their par value. The study shows that the total loss at current prices (taken in October 1996) over the highest price recorded by these companies is about Rs. 14,000 crore.

High pricing of public issues during the period under study was not justified. In most of the cases, the pricing was manipulated by merchant-bankers who were keen to some how sell the issue to the public."[12]

Even though, the issuer has the power to appoint the various intermediaries in the new issue function, but the actual work performed by the intermediaries like brokers, underwriters, registrar to issue and collecting banker is based on the able guidance and supervision of the merchant-bankers.

To extract the proper work from the various other intermediaries in the new issue management is a problem to the merchant-bankers. Therefore, how far the merchant-banker has succeeded in his operation to get the work from the intermediaries is to be studied.

There are plenty of merchant-bankers in the new issue market. But all of them are not having adequate infrastructure facilities to manage the new issues. In spite of all these shortcomings, the merchant-bankers are floating a number of new issues. All these problems may lead to poor performance of the merchant-bankers. Hence, there is a need for scientific enquiry to probe empirically the good and bad performance of the merchant-bankers.

Therefore, it has raised the following questions in the minds of the researcher as well as one who evinces interest in merchant banking industry. (1) What are the functions involved in the new issue management services? (2) Does SEBI regulate the merchant banking industry adequately? (3) What are the Challenges to the lead merchant-bankers while rendering the lead management services? (4) How do the lead merchant-bankers protect the interest of the investor?

Therefore, the survey of "New Issue Management Services by Lead Merchant-bankers in India" is of particular interest both to the investors as well as to the merchant-bankers. This fact finding study is conducted on merchant banking organisations in India to identify the above mentioned problems related to the new issue management services of merchant-banker and to find out some solutions.

Review of Literature

There are many studies conducted on new issue market and Merchant Banking. But there is a paucity of empirical studies in the new issue management services of merchant-bankers in India. A brief review of literature relating to new issue market and merchant banking is presented in the following paragraphs.

B. Bhatia's (1976) study on the "New Issue Market of India" has traced the development of institutions and policies relating to capital market. The trends in the new issue market between 1958–1973 have been analysed. It also considers the cost of floatation of issue of equity and preference shares between new and existing companies. The analysis was based on prospectus of 570 new companies and 110 existing companies which entered into the capital market during 1958–73. The major findings were: (1) Half of the companies issued only equity shares and one-fourth issued both equity and preference shares. (2) About 48 per cent of new equity issues was placed outside the public market. (3) The average cost of flotation of equity issues of new companies was more than the existing companies.

Khan's (1977 and 1978) fairly comprehensive work on new issue market was based on the sample consisting of 208 companies listed in the Bombay Stock Exchange. The study observed that capital issues were more important form of finance to the progressive companies during the 13 years period. Old companies have got more support from the new issue market than the new companies, particularly in the period 1968–73. The magnitude of financing by new issue market of old companies was twice that of new companies.

Gujarati (1981) in his doctoral dissertation on "Performance of New Equity Shares: An Indian Experience" examined the question of the risk adjusted return in the new issue market. His conclusion was that investors in the new issue market in 1970's earned nearly 2 per cent per month.

Verma, J.C. (1989) in his Ph.D. thesis on "The Organisation and Management of Merchant banking" revealed the evolution of merchant banking, organisational pattern of the merchant banking, services of the merchant-banker and the merchant-banker impact on the capital restructuring.

Agarwal (1997) who published his thesis on "New Issue Market operations in India" discussed the conceptual legal and policy framework of governing the New Issue Market. He also critically examined the measures taken by SEBI in the New Issue Market, its role towards investor protection and highlighting the drawbacks and practices in the New Issue Market.

Madhusoodanan and Thiripalraju M. (1997) in their study on "Under pricing in Initial Public Offerings: The Indian Evidence" examine the price behaviour of Indian IPOs in the short–run as well as in the long–run perspectives. They also analyse the performance of Merchant-bankers in terms of pricing of issues.

Meenakshisundaram, R. (1997) unpublished thesis on "Services of Merchant-bankers—A study with reference to new issues management" examined the services of the merchant-bankers with reference to new issue management from the investors' point of view. It was made using the sample survey method. Some of the findings of the study were: (1) The merchant-bankers in India are performing varied services, they are found to have a marked preference for new issues management and underwriting (2) The three roles played by merchant-bankers as Lead Managers, Co–managers and Advisors, in which their preference is to be lead managers. (3) The nationalised banks have played a dominant role as Lead Managers. (4) Direct procurement was the dominant method of securing business for the merchant-bankers. (5) The majority of investors, experienced lack of liquidity and absence of scope for making reasonable gain by liquidating their holding at a later date. (6) Among the various factors influencing the investors decisions in subscribing to the primary issue, "the past financial performance of the company", "the promoters' competence" and "the quality of management" have emerged as the dominant factors.

Manas Pandey (1997) published thesis on "New Issue Market Management of India" examined the regulatory framework governing the operations of NIM along with the volume and dispersals of new issues for financing of the corporate enterprises in India. Some of the suggestions of the study were: (1) To devise measures to setting up of independent

Merchant Banks in the country is urgently needed. (2) To devise measures for setting up of independent underwriting houses for small security issues. (3) The consortium of underwriting should be developed for investigating into the viability of the project and distribution of securities on regional basis. (4) In order to control the cost of issues, the standard norms should be fixed up irrespective of the size of the issues.

Objectives

The broad objectives of the present study are outlined as under:

1. to identify the functional activities of issue management and new issue management services undertaken by the merchant-bankers.
2. to study the organisational structure and the general profile of the merchant-bankers.
3. to assess the functioning of the merchant-bankers in the pre-issue and post-issue management phases.
4. to evaluate the new issue performance of the merchant-bankers, and
5. to examine the reactions of the lead merchant-bankers towards the measures of the SEBI and Stock Exchanges.

Scope of the Study

1. *Selection of Activities*

The Category I merchant-banker (Lead Merchant-banker) can act as an issue manager, advisor, consultant, underwriter and portfolio manager. Among the above activities the issue manager's function is a vital one, shouldering the entire responsibility of the issue management function. Hence, the researcher has taken only the lead merchant-bankers' issue management function for the present study.

2. *Period Covered*

This study embraced a period of 6 years i.e. from 1991–92 to 1996–97 and in case of primary data the period concentrated two financial years namely 1995–96 and 1996–97.

3. *Area of the Study*

The present study is focused on the new issue management services of merchant-bankers in all the zones of the country, comprising of Tamilnadu, Andhra Pradesh, Maharashtra, Delhi, Kerala, West Bengal and Uttar Pradesh (see Exhibit). The location of the sampled merchant-bankers in zone-wise and institutions-wise is given in Annexure IX.

Hypotheses

1. There is no significant difference in the performance of the merchant-bankers who have handed issues after SEBI's entry norms (Minimum three years track record of payments) from those who have handled issues before such norms of SEBI.
2. There is no significant difference in the performance of the Private sector merchant-bankers who have handled issues with the performance of the Public sector merchant-bankers who have handled issues, and
3. There is no significant difference in the performance of the multiple merchant-bankers who have handled issues collectively with the performance of the single merchant-banker who have handled issues solely.

Definition of the Concepts

New Issues

It means offers to the general public, the equity shares or bonds by companies already existing, or new companies being formed and also by the public sector units, government bodies etc. for the first time.

New Issues Market

It is the issue market which deals with the raising of fresh capital by companies that encompasses all institutions dealing in issues.

New Issue Management Services

These services usually entail the management of a new issue on behalf of a corporate client or an institution, the origination, underwriting and distribution and all other administrative work in connection with the new issues.

AREA OF THE STUDY

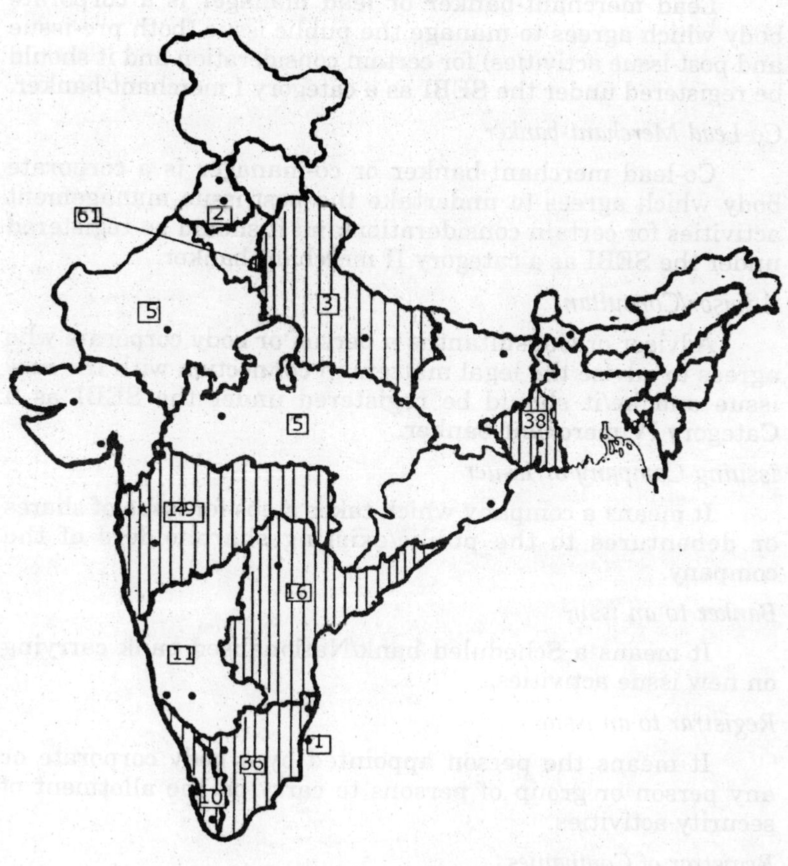

Scale 1: 17,000,000 1 cm = 170 kms

• refers to Place of Stock Exchanges (Non–screen based)

▭ refers to Number of Category I Merchant Bankers.

▥ refers to Area of the Study

* refers to Screen based Stock Exchanges

Lead Merchant-banker

Lead merchant-banker or lead manager is a corporate body which agrees to manage the public issue (both pre-issue and post-issue activities) for certain consideration and it should be registered under the SEBI as a category I merchant-banker.

Co-Lead Merchant-banker

Co-lead merchant-banker or co-manager is a corporate body which agrees to undertake the post-issue management activities for certain consideration and it should be registered under the SEBI as a category II merchant-banker.

Advisor/Consultant

Advisor or Consultant is a person or body corporate who agrees to advise the legal matters in connection with the new issue and he/it should be registered under the SEBI as a Category IV merchant-banker.

Issuing Company or Issuer

It means a company which takes steps for issue of shares or debentures to the public/existing shareholders of the company.

Banker to an issue

It means a Scheduled bank/Nationalised bank carrying on new issue activities.

Registrar to an issue

It means the person appointed by a body corporate or any person or group of persons to carry on the allotment of security activities.

Registrar of Companies

It is one among the regulating authorities of companies. All the companies should register their name with the Registrar of Companies.

Private Sector Merchant-banker

It is organised for undertaking the merchant banking business by the stock brokers or consultancies.

Public Sector Merchant-banker

Private Sector Banks, Financial Institutions and Nationalised Bank have formed either subsidiary or division for undertaking merchant banking business.

Private Sector Bank

A Public limited banking company one which is not owned by the central or state or both.

Promoter

A person one who takes necessary step to form a company.

Underwriter

The person who gives a guarantee to purchase stocks or bonds that remain unsold after public issue.

At Discount

A security which is issued at a price lower than its face value.

At Par

When a company issue its shares at a price equal to the face value are said to have been issued at par.

At Premium

A price higher than the face value at which a company makes a public issue of its share or debenture.

Share Broker

A share broker is an agent acting as an intermediary between an issuer and an investor for which he receives commission called brokerage.

Principal Officer

A director in a merchant banking organisation, who is responsible for new issue management activities.

Debt–Equity Ratio

Ratio that measures a company's financial leverage, that is the total amount owned to outsiders (Debt) divided by the funds provided by stockholders (equity).

Earnings Per Share

Amount of profit earned by a company less than attributable to the shareholders divided by the number of ordinary share which have been used.

Effectiveness of Merchant Banking Services

The over all performance of a merchant banking organisation from the viewpoint of value of the output that is the post-issue performance of new issues.

Issue Price

A company makes a public issue at premium or par or discount value.

Market Price

The Price at which a security was bought or sold on a particular day.

Fundamentals

The company's present, anticipated financial position and prospects of the concerned industry is known as fundamentals.

Infrastructure

It respects to network of information and controls, rules, regulations and procedures, decision-making mechanisms, authority relationship etc.

Listing

Admission of security (Shares or debentures) of a public limited company on a recognized stock exchange which provides a forum for the purchase and sale of securities.

Lock-in-Period

Period up to which an Investor/Promoter is refrained from selling the security.

Performance Analysis

Review of data on new issue to make comparisons, evaluate performance and recommend improvements for a merchant banking organisation.

Methodology

The present study is based on survey method and it is explorative in nature. It is mainly based on the primary sources. It is supported by the questionnaire. The questionnaire was mailed to the sampled units. The researcher in some cases visited the sampled units directly with the questionnaire. Before finalising the questionnaire, a pilot study was made on 4

Merchant-bankers in September 1996 at Hyderabad. A rough questionnaire was pretested. On the basis of experience the questionnaire had to be revised and improved. The revised questionnaire was circulated among the Merchant-bankers during May-September 1997.

Sample Frame

The primary data were collected by adopting the stratified sampling techniques:

Selection of Category: There are four categories of merchant-bankers in the field. As on 30.06.1995 as per SEBI's data source, the distribution of 4 categories was as follows: Category I–357, Category II–37, Category III–135 and Category IV–317.

The total number of merchant-bankers was 846. The researcher has confined his study only to Category I merchant-banker.

Selection of Number of Category I Merchant-bankers

A list of merchant-bankers was obtained from SEBI office. As per SEBI's data source there are 357 category I Lead merchant-bankers. However during 1995-96, all the category I merchant-bankers did not undertake new issue business. There were only 261 units which actively involved in the issue management business. Therefore, the researcher decided to take up 10 per cent of the sample from 261 active units. The sample of 26 merchant-bankers have been drawn on stratified basis based on Table 1 stratification. The list of the sampled merchant-bankers are presented in the Annexure X.

The secondary data were gathered from the following sources:

(*a*) Publication of SEBI, RBI, Stock Exchanges, Ministry of Finance, Company Law Board, Company News and Notes and Registrar of Companies.

(*b*) Journals, books, manuals, monographs, Newspapers and magazines.

(*c*) Company prospectus, Annual reports and Financial statements of merchant-bankers.

Table 1.1: Sample Selection of Category I Lead Merchant Bankers

	Segmentation of Lead Merchant Bankers	*Active**	*Sample*
(i)	All India Financial Institutions	7	1
(ii)	State Financial Institutions and Industrial Development Institutions	10	1
(iii)	Nationalised Banks	20	2
(iv)	Subsidiaries of Nationalised Banks	5	1
(v)	Private Sector Banks	12	2
(vi)	Foreign Banks	6	—
(vii)	Private Merchant Bankers	201	19
	Total	261	26

Source: *The Merchant Banker Update July 1996, p. 44.

Samples for analysis of the Issue statistics of the sampled merchant-bankers have been taken from the total population of corporate enterprises which came out with public issues during 1.4.1995 to 31.3.1997. These issues were handled by the sample merchant-bankers under study. All these issues were equity shares.

Samples for the new issue performance have been selectively taken from the total population of Corporate enterprises which came out with public issues during the 6 months from 1.1.96 to 30.6.96. These issues were handled by both the sample merchant-bankers under study and other merchant-bankers.

The market price of the issues after the listing of one year, as published in the Express Investment Week from 30th December 1996-5th January 1997 to 23-29th June 1997 has been taken as the base. Gains and losses, computed as on the cut off period of issues after one year, has not been annualised. Issues which are quoting at issue price have been placed in a separate category as there is neither gain nor loss to the investor. The number of companies which has made public issues during 1.1.96 to 30.6.96 period amounted to 762. All these shares were equity shares.

For the testing of hypotheses, the premium issues made during 6 months from 1.1.96. to 30.6.1996 were considered. The total number of companies taken as sample for testing the hypothesis was 25. The names of the 25 companies and the names of the corresponding lead merchant-bankers and the issues price and the market price are given in the Annexure XI. For the purpose of this analysis, the merchant-bankers who are taken as samples, have been classified into three groups as datewise, segmentwise and participationwise. Datewise group is again classified into Issues before entry norms of SEBI and after entry norms of SEBI. Segmentwise group is classified into Public sector and Private Sector. Participationwise group is classified as Single and Multiple.

Techniques of Collection of Data

Collection of Data

The present study is mainly based on the primary sources. It is supported by the questionnaire. The questionnaire was mailed to the sampled units. The researcher in some cases visited the sampled units directly with the questionnaire. Before finalising the questionnaire, a pilot study was made on 4 Merchant-bankers in September 1996 at Hyderabad. A rough questionnaire was pre-tested. On the basis of experience the questionnaire had to be revised and improved. The revised questionnaire was circulated among the Merchant-bankers during May-September 1997.

The questionnaire was mailed to all the category I Merchant-bankers. The researcher received 17 filled-in questionnaires. During the collection period, the primary market was sluggish and some of merchant-bankers closed down their offices and the questionnaires were returned to the researcher. Hence, the researcher was constrained to adhere to the 10 per cent sample of the Category I merchant-bankers. Since the response rate was poor (65.38), efforts were made by the researcher by sending the questionnaires repeatedly. The researcher again received 4 filled-in questionnaires. Finally, the researcher personally made a visit to the merchant-bankers offices to collect the required number of the questionnaires.

During the personal contact with the merchant-bankers some of the managers of the merchant-bankers hesitated to disclose all the details in the questionnaire. Yet another group of managers declined to answer any question and did not co-operate with the researcher. However, these difficulties were overcome by persistent effort and by creating a rapport with merchant-bankers.

Analysis of Data

The data collected were tabulated and presented in the appropriate places in various chapters. Diagrams, charts and graphs have also been used. While analysing the quantitative data, statistical techniques like averages, index number, standard deviation, correlation coefficient, student t-test etc., have been computed and used.

For testing the hypotheses the co-efficient of correlation was computed as an index of the degree of association between the issue price (IP) and market price (MP). The IP differs from company to company. As such if any comparison is to be made on the deviation between the IP and MP the same has to be adjusted for issue price differences. Hence, researcher computed a relative deviation in IP from that of the MP. This is given by the formula:

$$\text{Relative Deviation (rd)} = \text{Issue Price (IP)} - \frac{\text{Market Price (MP)}}{\text{Issue Price (IP)}}$$

The relative deviation was computed for all the companies under the sample. The mean values of relative deviation was computed separately. The difference in means was tested for statistical significance using t-test. If the observed deviation in mean value is greater than the acceptance limit under t-test, null hypothesis is rejected.

Wherever, multiple responses are obtained from merchant-bankers an attempt is made to arrange responses in order of priority. For this purpose, the respondents were asked to indicate their preferences in 1, 2, 3, 4, 5, 6, 7 and 8 among the multiple responses given by them. The average weighted scores were computed by assigning weights as 8, 7, 6, 5, 4, 3, 2 and 1 to preferences. The weighted scores are obtained by multiplying the number of respondents preferring a rank with the respective weight. Final ranks are given to the weighted scores. The data is interpreted in terms of the ranks assigned by this method.

Limitation

The following are some of the limitations for the study:

While some companies were good enough to supply their Balance-Sheets/Financial details, many have chosen not to supply. Therefore, it could not be possible to study the financial analysis.

Except a very few merchant-bankers, a large number of them did not maintain separate details about their issue management income as well as expenses. They could neither provide the details about the issuer nor they could furnish the necessary details about their own income in issue management, listing price, present condition of the project and other details. Therefore, the new issue performance of the merchant-bankers under study was based on the secondary sources.

The study was mainly confined to the public issue management services of the merchant-bankers that too in the equity issues. This study excluded the Rights Issue Management Function and Bond Issue Management Function in the Public Issue.

Except very few merchant-bankers, a large number of them did not disclose their performance regarding project appraisal, advisory service, bridge loan, term loan syndication and syndication of working capital.

Chapter Scheme

The first chapter deals with introduction, the chapter II "Services of Merchant Banking" describes the function of the new issue management. It outlines how the SEBI regulates the merchant-bankers in the new issues management. It also gives a brief account of the important services offered by the sampled units and the service charges for each service.

Chapter III "Merchant-bankers—General Profile" highlights the organisational structure of the merchant-bankers and employees strength and infrastructure facilities of the sampled merchant banking units.

Chapter IV "Analysis I—Pre-Issue Management" analyses the practical difficulties faced by the sample lead merchant-bankers while rendering the Pre-issue management services.

Chapter V "Analysis II—Post-Issue Management" describes the pragmatic problems faced by the sample lead merchant-bankers while rendering the Post-issue management services.

Chapter VI "Impact of SEBI Measures" describes the functional difficulties faced by the sampled lead merchant-bankers with Securities and Exchange Board of India, Stock Exchanges, Registrar of Companies etc.

Chapter VII "Merchant-bankers-Performance Analysis" deals with New Issue Performance of the sampled lead merchant-bankers.

Chapter VIII "Findings, Conclusion and Suggestions" presents the recapitulation of the entire thesis and the important findings of the study.

REFERENCES

1. A.E. Hart, *A Key to the Stock Exchange and Investments.* Blackie and Son Ltd. London, 1938, p. 77.
2. V.A. Avadhani, *Investment Management.* Himalaya Publishing House, Bombay, 1996, p. 141.
3. H.R. Machiraju, *Merchant Banking Principles and Practice.* New Age International (P) Limited Publishers, New Delhi, 1995, p. 115.
4. News Bureau, "Savings Rate up Marginally"...*The Economic Times,* 27th December, 1997, p. 1.
5. "The Hindu–Survey on Indian Industries 1995". *The Hindu,* 1996, p. 28.
6. L.M. Bhole, "The Indian Capital Market at Cross Roads" *Vikalpa* Vol. 20, No. 2 April–June, 1995 p. 30.
7. R.M. Srivastava, *Financial Management*, Pragathi Prakashan, Meerut, 1979, p. 445.
8. A.K. Sen Gupta, "Merchant banking: Some Issues I". *The Financial Express,* 17th January, 1991, p. 6.
9. Roy Pinto, "Of Bulls, bears and stags". *Business India,* 9th–22nd March, 1998, p. 179.

10. K. Sivakumar and Giri Venkatesan, "To ensure quality issues, merchant-bankers must lead from the front". *The Hindu Business Line,* 9th July, 1995, p. 20.

11. C.R.L. Narasimhan, "Aspects of primary market trauma". *The Hindu,* 23rd November, 1998, p. 19.

12. M.K. Venu, "Primary issues hit rock bottom in last two years: MOF". *The Economic Times* 13th January 1997, p. 9.

2

Services of Merchant Banking

Introduction

Merchant Banking service is the part of the financial services. Financial services would generally be either fund-based or fee-based services. Providing funds by way of loans, inter-corporate deposits, bills discounting, leasing and hire purchasing are some of the fund-based services. On the other hand, fee-based services involve issue management, acting as advisors/consultants, underwriters or portfolio managers. As far as India is concerned, there is no specialised or exclusive merchant banking service organisation. All the sample merchant banking organisations are mixed type they provide both the fee-based and fund-based services. Very recently, SEBI has restricted the merchant-bankers from doing the fund–based services. But there is no bar on providing underwriting and portfolio services under the separate registration with fee-based services. Therefore, the researcher briefly discusses all the financial services in brief and merchant banking services in detail. The financial services are broadly classified into the following heads: 1. Merchant Banking Services, 2. Corporate Advisory Services, 3. Investor Advisory Services, 4. Forex Advisory Services, 5. Corporate Financing Services and 6. Other Services.

Under the head Merchant banking services, the services such as Corporate structuring, Issue Management, Placement or Bought Out Deals, Bridge Loan, Loan Syndication, Syndication of working capital and Underwriting are included.

The Corporate Advisory services consist of Identification of projects, Arranging of Foreign Technical Collaborations, Advice on Company Law matters, SEBI and Securities and Contract Regulation matters, Acquisitions and Mergers, Project Appraisals, Project Certification, OTCEI Listings, Corporate Fund Management and Market making of debt securities. Investor Advisory services include Portfolio Management Services, OTCEI trading in securities, stock broking, fixed deposit mobilisation, Custodian Services, Registrar and Transfer Agents, Bankers to Issue, Marketing of Debt Instruments, Refund Banker to Issue, Operation of Investment facilitation centre and in publication of Investment News Magazines and Research. Forex Advisory Services normally include the following services: Services of Money Changers, Foreign Exchange Broking, Advice on Euro-Issues and NRI advisory services. Corporate Financing Services are the major services of the financial services organisations. They are: Leasing, Hire Purchasing, Bills Discounting, Inter-Corporate deposit mobilising, Factoring, Venture Capital Financing and Project Financing. Services like Housing Finance, Consumer Finance, etc., are the other services of the financial services organisations. Of all the above mentioned services, the merchant banking services are very much relevant to the present study. Therefore, the merchant banking services and the relative fees charged for that services by the study units are discussed in the following paragraphs. The financial services and merchant banking services are depicted in the form of a diagram in Diagram I and II.

Merchant Banking Services

At the outset, there are eight services offered by the Merchant-bankers. An issuer may need any of the service as and when the circumstances warrant.

Issue Management

The issue management involves varied functions. It starts with designing up the capital structure, type of issue instrument and ends with mobilisation of funds from the general public. The Ministry of Finance suggested lead Merchant-banker fees ranged between 0.20 per cent and 0.50 per cent of the issue price. But the fees are negotiated by the

DIAGRAM I
Financial Services

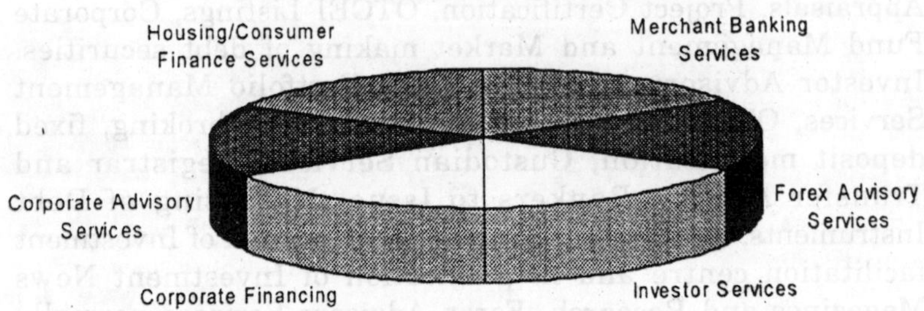

DIAGRAM II
Merchant Banking Services

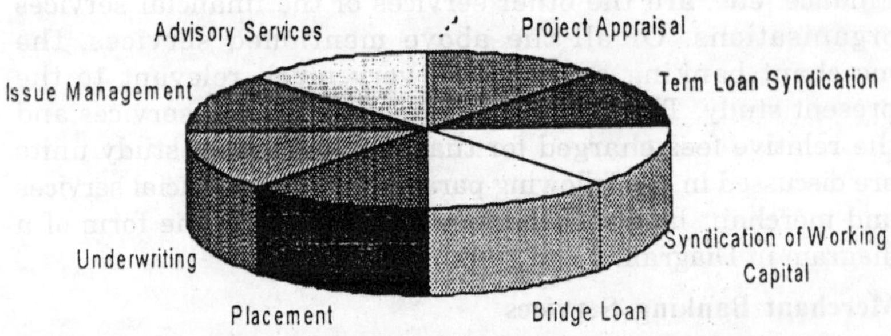

merchant-banker from the issuer. In practice, the lead manager fees ranges between 0.50 per cent and 2.00 per cent, and it should be mentioned in the offer documents. In case of more than one lead manager is to be appointed by the issuer, the total fees would be shared among the lead managers. The merchant-banker insists on the issuer to pay the issue management fees in different stages like receipt of issue mandate, SEBI approval, acknowledgement card and closure of the issue.

Underwriting

Underwriting is a contigent contract, whereby a person agrees to take up shares specified in the underwriting agreement if the public fails to subscribe for them. The person who assumes this risk is called "Underwriter" and such an arrangement is known as "Underwriting". The underwriter is eligible to receive the commission, whether he is called upon to take up shares or not. SEBI has allowed the merchant-bankers and registered underwriters to act as an underwriter.

It is mandatory on the part of the lead manager to shoulder the responsibility to accept a minimum underwriting obligation of 5 per cent of the total underwriting commitments or Rs. 25 lakhs whichever is less. The Ministry of Finance suggested underwriting commission for equity shares is 2.5 per cent for both public subscription and on devolvement. But underwriting commission is negotiated by the lead merchant-banker from the issuer. In practice, it ranges between 2.5 per cent and 5 per cent.

Project Appraisal

Project appraisal is the analysis of cost and benefit of a proposed project with the goal of assuring a rational allocation of limited funds among alternative investment opportunities in view of achieving certain specified goals. In the case of Project Appraisal, the merchant-banker undertakes detailed Techno-Economic Appraisal of Projects.

Formerly, the project appraisal service is provided by all the lead merchant-bankers. As per 1996 guidelines of the SEBI, the Financial Institutions and Scheduled Commercial Banks alone can provide this particular service and the appraising entity must contribute at least 5 per cent of the Company's project cost in the form of equity or debt. Therefore, this service is not provided by all the merchant-bankers.

Advisory Service

The merchant-bankers are assisting the issuer in deciding Promoters' contributions, the Debt/Equity Ratio, means of financing for the project and type(s) of instrument(s) for the issue. The minimum fees for the above services are between Rs. 25,000 and Rs. 1,00,000. All the study units are undertaking this service.

Bridge Loan

The bridge loans will be sanctioned by the merchant-banker themselves or making necessary arrangement with Financial Institutions or Investment Institutions or some times with the commercial banks. But at present the Nationalised bank based merchant-banker could not provide this service because the Reserve Bank of India has asked banks not to entertain with bridge financing. However the private merchant-banker can provide the bridge loan facilities based on the issuer strength of the project. The charge for the above service is 1 per cent of the finance arranged.

Placement

The merchant-bankers would assist the company on placement of the equity shares of the company on a preferential reservation/firm allotment basis with FIs/FIIs and Mutual Funds in accordance with the capital structure finanised for the issue. The charges for this service is 1.5 per cent of the Issue size.

Term Loan Syndication

Another very important service of the merchant-banker is the syndication of term loans. In this respect, the merchant-banker can assist the company in selection of the prospective Institutions and Banks likely to participate in financing.

Some of the merchant-bankers are arranging the deferred payment Guarantees apart from the syndication of terms loans. The charges for above services are 0.5 per cent for 5 crore loan syndicated or deferred payment guarantee arranged.

Most of the merchant-bankers are having the lease/hire purchase activities together with their merchant banking services. Hence, they may sometime arrange finance for the issuer through the lease/hire purchase syndication. The charges would be 1 per cent of the amount syndicated through the lease/hire purchase. All the sampled units are rendering these services.

Syndication of Working Capital

The Issuers sometime ask the merchant-bankers to arrange the working capital for both long-terms and short-term purposes. In this respect the merchant-bankers assist the company in determining its working capital requirements and placing the same with the consortium of banks, financial institutions or financiers, if necessary. The charges for the syndicating working capital requirements are 0.25 per cent for Rs. 5 crore working capital arranged. Some of the private merchant-bankers, banks and financial institutions of the study units are rendering this service.

Functions of New Issue Management

The functions of the new issue market can be classified into three categories namely 1. Origination, 2. Underwriting and 3. Distribution. Origination refers to the work of investigation and analysis and processing of new proposals. This is divided into preliminary investigation and advisory services to improve the quality of capital issues. This part of the work is undertaken by the merchant-bankers and advisors.

Underwriting entails an agreement whereby a person/ organisation agrees to take a specified number of shares or debentures or a specified amount of stock offered to the public in the event of the public not subscribing to it, in consideration of a commission called underwriting commission. In India, the underwriting tasks are undertaken by the institutional as well as non-institutional underwriters.

Distribution refers to the sale of securities to the ultimate investors. It is another important job which can be performed by brokers and dealers in securities who maintain regular and direct contact with the ultimate investors. A developed new issue market is characterised by the presence of specialised agencies to perform each of these three services. As far as India is concerned there are no specialised agencies to conduct all the three services. However, each service is quite distinct from the other, and is usually paid for separately by the issuing company.

Most of the merchant banking institutions are specialised in origination. However, some merchant banking institutions are combing two services such as origination with distribution, or origination with underwriting, or underwriting with distribution, while a few may engage in all the three.

Apart from the above general classification of new issue functions, in view of the lead managers it can be also classified into two namely (1) Pre-Issue management and (2) Post–Issue management. On the basis of this classification the researcher discusses the new issue function of the merchant-bankers in the following paragraphs.

Pre-Issue Management Function

1. Sources of Procurement

The issuer who intends to make a public issue, can make an enquiry to the merchant-banker. He sends a letter in this regard and shows his interest in making a public issue. He has a choice to send a requisition either to one merchant-banker or too many merchant-bankers. This is a direct approach. But sometime the merchant-banker may find out the intention of the issuer to making a public Issue through other sources like brokers, underwriters, advisors/consultants, project appraiser, leading institutions, clients and parent organisations of the merchant-banker.

2. Selection of Issuer

Once the intention of the company to go public is known, the merchant-banker either directly or through different sources, asks the promoters or the directors of the proposed company what are the requirements of Public issue. In this aspect, the merchant-banker puts reasons for the public issue. For that purpose the merchant-banker should ask the proposed company to submit three copies of the Memorandum and Articles of Association and the audited final accounts of past few years, if it is an existing company. By carefully analysing final accounts and documents the merchant-banker decides whether to accept the new issue proposal or not. It is his duty to assess and analyse the company, the product and the promoters before he accepts the assignment.

The merchant-banker's role in selecting the issuer is immense. The merchant-banker should take into consideration the type of industry, technical, marketing and economic feasibility of the project. Besides the feasibility of the project, the promoter's background and his contribution to the proposed project also should be taken into consideration by the merchant-banker before selection of the issuer. In this connection, the merchant-banker specified the statutory conditions and his own conditions to the issuer. If the issuer agrees to the conditions of the merchant-banker then he retains the merchant-banker for the issue.

Similarly, the lead manager of an issue can be finalised by the issuer based on so many factors such as ability to make arrangements of project finance, bridge loan, promoter's stake, minimum number of shareholders, completion of issue within a period etc.

3. Agreement with Issuer

Once the issuer agrees to appoint a lead manager, before entering into an agreement with issuer, the merchant-banker decides the charges for the issue management. The lead Merchant-banker fees ranges between 0.50 per cent and 2.00 per cent of the issue size. The fees are negotiated by the merchant-banker from the issuer. But it is mentioned in the offer documents.

After that the lead merchant-banker should enter into a Memorandum of Understanding (MOU) with the issuer company. In that agreement, the lead merchant-banker and issuer set out their mutual rights, liabilities and obligations relating to such issue and in particular to disclosures, allotment and refund.

When there is more than lead manager to the issue, they must enter into an Inter-se Allocation of Responsibilities (IAR) with clear demarcation of such responsibilities amongst themselves. In this respect the lead manager may accept any familiar work from the other lead manager.

4. Documentation

The first and foremost activity of the merchant-banker in the pre-issue management is the collection of various reports from the issuer. If the issuer has already prepared the documents and obtained various certificates, approvals from the authorities, the merchant-banker receives the same and scrutinises it thoroughly. If the issuer has not already prepared the documents and obtained certificates and approvals, the merchant-banker assist the issuer in this respect. In this connection, the lead merchant-banker makes a number of visits to the issuer premises or project site. The consultant and issuing company auditor is very helpful to the merchant-banker to obtain various documents from the issuer.

5. Appraisal/Assistance for Appraisal

The next important work of the merchant-banker is to appraise the project. If the merchant-banker is a financial institution or bank, he himself is empowered to appraise the project according to the SEBI norms. On the other hand, if he is not a banker or financial institution, he will assist the company to send the project report for appraisal to financial institutions or banks. In the former case, he is going to contribute at least 5 per cent of project cost in the form of Debt or Equity. Before submitting the project for the appraisal, the merchant-banker should scrutinize it properly and the lead merchant-banker appraises the project in financial institution's or from bank's angle.

6. Arrangement of Project Finance

The merchant-bankers have to arrnage the financier on behalf of promoter for the success of the issue. Some merchant-bankers themselves provide money through different route to the issuer for the success of the public issue. Further, the Banks and Financial Institutions' based merchant-bankers, due to their money power, term-lending relationships with the corporate clients are in a position to arrange project finance and attract the promoters to award the issue mandates to them or their subsidiaries.

7. Due Diligence Certificate

The most important work of the merchant-banker is the preparation of due diligence certificate. It is the legal obligation on the part of Lead Merchant-banker. As per the due diligence certificate, the lead merchant-banker of any issue has to give an undertaking that he has examined various documents, including those relating to litigation like commercial disputes, patent disputes, disputes with collaboration etc., and other information in connection with filing of the draft prospectus. Therefore, the head merchant-banker ensures that all the relevant information have been disclosed in prospectus. The lead manager should ensure that the audited statement and unaudited statement particulars contained in the prospectus should not be more than six months old from the issue opening date. Even though, there is more than one lead manager in an issue but all the documentation work is done by any one lead manager subject to the inter-se allocation of responsibilities of the merchant-bankers. The merchant-banker depends on the issuer, company auditor, secretary, legal advisor and bankers to the company, and Registrar of Companies for the preparation of the due diligence certificate.

8. Vetting of Prospectus

The sincere and the most critical part of the work of the merchant-banker is the preparation of the draft prospectus and vetting of prospectus. The lead manager prepares a draft prospectus of the company incorporating all the details regarding promoters, the company, the main objects, the project details, the listing particulars, the capital structure of the company. It also includes date of allotment of shares to the promoters before the public issue, the lock-in-period for promoters share, terms of payment of the issue, application procedure, cost of project and means of finance, promoters equity stake after the present issue, past financial performance of the company if any (audited). Then lead manager submits it to the SEBI with all the enclosures and details etc., on behalf of the issuer for getting the approval from SEBI.

Formerly, as per the SEBI regulation the issuer must submit to SEBI the draft prospectus along with the Due Diligence Certificate, Inter-se allocation of responsibilities and Memorandum of Understanding with the lead managers for vetting, at least 15 days before filing with Registrar of Companies. The SEBI authorities scrutinise the draft prospectus thoroughly and make some observations or comments or objections and report the issuer accordingly. These things are duly considered by the issuer and he has to make necessary changes in the final copy. Finally, the SEBI issues an Acknowledgement Card to the issuer if all the corrections are carried out or complied with by the issuer. The Card is valid for three months. This is a hectic process to the merchant-bankers and it will consume the major part of work and time of the new issue process. This has been the practice of the SEBI from 1992 onwards. But suddenly it has decided to stop vetting the Rights offer issue in the year 1995. Later SEBI has decided to stop vetting offer documents for public issue also from 10th December, 1996.

9. Selection of Intermediaries

No doubt, in the new issue management service the merchant-banker occupies a pivotal position in the whole new issue exercise. There are numerous other intermediaries like Registrar to the Issue, Underwriter, Broker, Sub-broker, Collecting Banker/agent, Refunding Banker, Printer, Advertiser, etc., involving the new issue work. The merchant-banker can assist the issuer company in selection of other intermediaries like Registrar to the Issue, Underwriter, Banker to the Issue, Broker, Printers etc.

(a) *Registrar to the Issue*

As per the SEBI's public issue requirements, a registrar to the issue registered with SEBI shall be appointed in all public issues. The "Registrars to the issue" or "Issue House" are responsible normally for receiving the share applications from various collection centres through controlling branches of Bankers to the issue, analysing them, recommending the basis of allotment in consultation with the Lead Managers to the Regional Stock Exchange for approval, arranging for despatch of allotment letters and preparing the Register of members etc. Registrar's job normally starts with the opening of the subscription list, and continues till the share certificates are despatched, and the Registrar of members along with other related Registers/details are handed over to the Company. The SEBI has two categories of Registrar and Transfer Agents. Category I agents can act as registrar to issues and handle share transfer work of companies. Those agents designated as Category II are either only registrars to issue or share transfer agents. The Lead Merchant-banker considers the registrar to the issue and evaluate it's infrastructure facilities for the new issue management.

(b) *Underwriter*

SEBI has allowed the merchant-bankers and registered underwriters to act as a underwriter. Investment Companies and Trusts, large firms of Stock Brokers, Commercial Banks, Life Insurance Corporation, Unit Trust of India, Industrial Credit and Investment Corporation of India, Industrial Development Bank of India, Industrial Finance Corporation also took up underwriting activity. But the lead manager(s) must satisfy themselves about the net worth of the underwriters and the outstanding commitments and disclose the same to SEBI. The number of underwriters for the issue would be decided by the issuer.

(c) Bankers to the Issue

The Ministry of Finance, by a notification in 1990, made it mandatory for the issuers to open collection centres at 57 centres. These centres are known as "Mandatory Centres". They include State Capitals, Recognised Stock Exchange Centres and other cities having population of more than 5 lakhs as per 1981 census. But SEBI has in its circular No 3(93)94 of 11th October 1993, addressed to all merchant-bankers has stipulated the inclusion of at least 30 mandatory centres as against 57, presently, which should include all the stock exchange centres. As an additional facility, the issuer in consultation with the lead manager appoints authorised collection agents and necessary disclosures should be made in the offer documents. The bankers to the issue are the commercial banks which will receive the share application money along with the share application forms from the prospective investors.

Depending upon the size of the issue at least 4 to 5 banks are designated as bankers to the Issue. Different branches of these banks are named at various locations where such application money is accepted. The branches are called collecting branches. The progress of the daily collections and the receipt of the share applications are reported by the these collecting branches to the controlling branch of the bank and also to the registrar to the issue. The lead merchant-bankers monitor the daily totals of applications received. The subscription list should be kept open for a minimum period of 3 working days. Depending upon the subscription level, the issuer will decide to close the subscription on the earliest date of closure or extend the date on the advice of the lead manager/

Registrar to the issue. The merchant-banker can consider bank to be appointed as Bankers to the issue and evaluate their branch network. The mandatory collection centres should include the places where regional stock exchanges function. By way of additional facility the company may appoint authorised collection agents, which shall be disclosed in the prospectus.

(d) Broker

The lead managers will acquaint with the prospective brokers about the issue by sending draft prospectus and obtain their consents to act as brokers to the issue, a copy of which is also delivered to the registrar of companies

(e) Printers

In consultation with the lead managers to the issue appointment or the selection of the printers to print the prospectus, application forms and other issue materials are finalised. Since the magnitude of the printing job will be massive, care should be taken that the printer concerned has adequate facilities to deliver the printed material in time and the capacity to execute the order for printing a large quantity of materials within a short time.

The lead manager seeks to convince the other intermediaries and procure the consent from them for the success of the issue. Some merchant banking outfits are rendering services like registrar to the issue, collecting banker, refund banker, underwriting, stock broking etc., apart from their merchant banking services. It is quite natural, the lead merchant-banker prefer to appoint the sister concern or concern did favour previously to lead merchant-banker.. But the selection of the intermediaries based on the principle of the quality of service, commitment to the service competitive cost and infrastructure facilities. The chart I shows the new issue management functionaries.

10. Assistance to Obtain Consents or Approvals

The apex body to control the new issue is the SEBI. Apart from the SEBI, the merchant-banker has to obtain the various approvals from Stock Exchanges, Reserve Bank of India,

Department of Company Affairs, Registrar of Companies etc. on behalf of the issuer. The SEBI officials after receiving the draft offer document critically scrutinise the details of the prospectus, major disclosures required for public awareness withheld on the document etc., and call for clarification/ resubmissions of the draft by the company. If SEBI is satisfied with the form and contents of the draft, either it issues acknowledgement card or on certain conditions acknowledges or raises objection on the draft prospectus.

Therefore, the draft prospectus has to be amended accordingly as instructed by the SEBI to get their acknowledgement card and has to be submitted with the Regional Stock Exchange authorities for approval. After getting approval letter from the stock exchange the draft prospectus with all its material documents and enclosures has to be submitted with the Registrar of Companies of that region for approval or acknowledgement card within one year from the date of SEBI's observation letter. The lead merchant-bankers write to the respective stock exchanges and seek their approval for appointment of their members as brokers/underwriters to the issue and also seek their requirement of number of copies of prospectus and application form for free distribution to their members.

In some cases, alteration or amendment in the Memorandum and Articles of Association of the company has to be approved by the stock exchange authorities where the shares of the company is proposed to be listed. Thus, the lead merchant-bankers have to maintain very close liaison with a number of government and semi-government bodies.

11. Pricing the Issue

The SEBI, the regulatory body has issued certain guidelines to be observed by companies issuing capital. (see Annexure XII—guidelines). As per these guidelines the following issues can be freely priced.

1. Issue by new companies being set up by the existing companies with a five-year track record of consistent dividend payment. The participation of promoting company should be less than 50 per cent of the

equity of the new company and the issue price must be made applicable to all the investors uniformly.

2. First issue by existing private/closely held company's with a 3 years track record of consistent dividend payment.
3. The existing listed companies can freely price the issues provided the prospectus must provide adequate information about the justification of the premium.

This should include the Net Asset Values as per the last audited Balance Sheet, premium according to the CCI formula and high and low prices of share for the last two years in case of a listed company. "CCI priced the new issues of capital by existing companies on the basis of average of their networth per share and profit earning capacity per share. The pricing policy of the CCI had been unduly conservative and had valued shares far below the ruling market price."[1]

As per the SEBI guidelines, the issuers can price their share according to their wish. But they have to give a justification as to the price and give sufficient disclosure in the prospectus. Therefore, pricing of an issue is more complicated. In this respect, the merchant-banker advises the issuer. Normally, the offer price is decided by a mutual discussion but very often the issuer wants to fix up the highest price which may not be possible to fetch in the prevailing market. At this juncture, the merchant-banker explains the issuer the market sentiment and suggests the price at which the issue may be acceptable to the market. At the same time, the merchant-bankers must see to it that they price the issue reasonably so as to give maximum appreciation from the investors. Therefore, they must take into account the factors such as promoter's track report, industry type, earning per share, fundamentals, CCI formula, market sentiments etc., and should not price the issue primarily on the basis of Market Value. Some other consideration in pricing is the capital issue shall be made fully paid up within 12 months from the date of closure of the issue. Minimum number of shares for which application is to be made shall be 200 shares of the face value of Rs. 10 each. Where the issue is at a premium the amount payable in all by each applicant shall not be less than Rs. 5000 irrespective of the size of the premium.

The lead manager can attract the investor by way of offering some sweeteners or make arrangement of safety net scheme. Sweeteners means the issuer offering instant advantage at the time of the issue opens like tax advantage, warrants and other benefits. Another new technique to attract the investors and improve the products is the safety net. This technique will develop in due course wherein the merchant-bankers assures the investors that he would buy back the shares at the issue price within a stipulated time. But any safety net scheme or buy back arrangements of the shares proposed in any public issue should be finalised in advance and disclosed.

12. Marketing Strategies

"Efficient Marketing of an issue determines the success of any public issue. Marketing of public issue is an art, however only strong issues can be the favourite of the investing public, which in turn becomes a great success by the efforts of the merchant-banker and the agencies involved in the issue".[2]

The first step to successful marketing of an issue is the choice of the method of marketing securities. There are generally three types of solicitations as methods of marketing securities. They are: (i) Direct Placement (ii) Investment Intermediaries and (iii) Underwriting.

In the case of direct placement, the application forms with a detailed report are mailed to the investors directly. If the issuer already had a good amount of branch network, he will directly approach the prospective investors through their branch network, utilising the services of the branches. The institutions such as Financial Institutions, Foreign Institutional Investors, Mutual Funds, Non Resident Indians and Overseas Corporate Bodies can be approached with the objective of tying up of firm allotments. This kind of firm allotments not only assure the selling but also attract the small investors to the market.

The proper method of reaching the investor is through the brokers and sub-brokers network. The merchant-banker has developed the broker network painstakingly over a long period of time. The merchant-banker together with the issuer can make the presentation about the project. The presentation highlighting the project and product should be made to the brokers at conferences and one-to-one meetings. With the help of issuers, the merchant-bankers design lucrative incentive schemes like target linked gift (kitty), free foreign travel and prizes, so as to attract the brokers and sub-brokers to push their issues successfully.

Proper allocation of underwriting is another step towards effective marketing. Distribution of underwriting is to be done on the basis of the performance and networth of each broker. It should be ensured that the entire amount available for underwriting is widely distributed among a large number of brokers. For this purpose, a sharply focused presentation of the issue should be prepared, by the lead merchant-banker for presentation to institutions and individuals. Apart from the above techniques the lead merchant-banker also depends on the techniques like Pre-writing the issue, Gray market operations, etc.

Under Pre-writing the issue, the lead manager along with the promoters, conducts road shows across the country, inviting high net worth individuals, brokers, corporate, etc., asking them to invest in the issue. If they decided on to apply, the lead merchant-banker will obtain a pre-writing commitment from them, and as per the agreement, they will have to deposit a cheque and application one day before the issue opens.

In gray market operations, promoters have an arrangement with brokers to offer a buy back at a price which is higher than the offered price or, in other words, an artificial premium is injected into the scrip of the proposed issue. At the time of the issue investors are interested in applying for the issue because the scrip is already commanding a premium in the market and they are assured a particular level of return in advance. This way the response of investors is evoked and the issue gets subscribed in the market. It is not a right marketing technique but it is practised by private merchant-bankers.

13. Publicity Campaign

The company in consultation with the lead manager plans its advertising campaign for the public issue and appoints an advertising agency. The advertising agencies have greater role to play in the preparation of advertisement copy. Success of an issue depends on the size of the advertisement media, frequency and the placement of the advertisement.

The first work of an advertising agency is to make statutory advertisements. The statutory issue advertisements namely 'issue open today' and 'issue closes today' have to be according to SEBI guidelines and stock exchange rules and regulations. The advertisement shall not state that the issue has been fully subscribed or over subscribed during the period when the issue is open. No announcement regarding closure of the issue shall be made except on the last closing date.

The other advertisement campaign involves Press releases, sponsorship of events, radio or T.V. advertisements, interviews in the media etc. They are aimed at building up public awareness of the company's performance and product. This could be followed by Press Conferences, tete-a-tete with important potential investors, site visits to the project, letters to shareholders of group companies, corporate advertisements etc. Previously the SEBI had a ban on the Corporate Advertisement. But the new clarification of the SEBI allows "any corporate body, which is desirous of making a public issue of securities, may issue corporate advertisements after 21 days from the date of the filing of the offer document with SEBI till the closure of the issue."[3] The Corporate advertisement includes risk factors, financial aspects, technical details, management background and other commercial details. But if any advertisement carries any financial data it should also contain data for the past three years and shall include key financial particulars. The company shall give an undertaking to the lead managers that it would not release information which is not contained in the offer documents. The company will obtain approval from the lead managers in respect of all issue advertisements and publicity materials. Some of the Unique Selling Propositions (USPs) of the company need to be highlighted. This includes export tie-ups technical collaboration, financial collaboration and any other USPs.

Before finalising the advertising campaign it is important to decide on the target segment of investors. To attract retail investors, generally the print media and bill boards are widely used. However, the most effective way to market an issue is through conferences, press briefing and open invitation, seminars, beside the word of mouth.

Deciding the venue of the conferences, travel plan of key persons, arranging the brochures (printed in regional languages), availability of application forms, working out the logistics for the senior management. So that they remain present at most of the conferences, etc., are complex functions and require skill and experiences. The merchant-banker plays the role of a guide by helping in the choice of media, determining the size and also the publications in which the advertisements should appear.

14. Fixing the Timing of the Issue

The time is the most crucial aspect in the marketing of the issue. It mostly depends on the general sentiments of the stock market. In the normal course, the timing is the essence of any marketing strategy. However, in Indian conditions one may not have the flexibility of waiting for favourable stock market conditions to launch an issue since the permission from the SEBI and other authorities may expire. Subscription for public issue should e kept open for at least 3 working days and a total period of not exceeding 10 working days are disclosed in the prospectus. The acknowledgement card issued by SEBI is valid for a period of one year i.e. issue opening date shall be within 365 days from the date of the observation letter is issued.

Regardless, it is important to time the issue as best as possible within the operating constraints. As far as timing is concerned there are some unique characteristics of the Indian Primary Market. They are:

(*a*) Festival Seasons, that is October and November.

(*b*) Vacation periods that is May and June.

(*c*) Tax payment period, that is March and April, and

(*d*) Refunds from Mega Issues.

Festival seasons, vacation and tax payment periods generally not desirable. But at the same time, during the tax payment period, the tax saving scheme or special tax benefit scheme can invoke interest to invest the money into the new issues. The bonus and dividend payment period of the companies also create an interest to the investors as well as the industrial workers to purchase the shares and debentures of the companies. The merchant-banker sometime can paly with the psychology of the investors. When the mega issues get highly oversubscribed refunds give the investors more money. Therefore, many small capital issues can plan their offerings around this time.

Due to prolonged bear phase, persistent need for funds and expiry of the period of the card, the issuer may not have much choice. But care must be taken to see to it that no other mega issue coincided with the mega issue. Also the issue date must be determined in such a way that the issue is closed before the mega issue's shares get listed. Here again the human psychology plays a role. If one mega issue gets listed at a discount to the offer price, naturally the investors do not tend to subscribe the other mega issue just open in the market. Therefore, the issue should not coincide with the other issue. Another important point is, if the one type industry issue gets under subscription recently, the issuer from the same industry must defer the issue for the time being. Hence, the issuer and the lead manager decide the opening and closing date of the issue. Then, the lead manager should communicate to stock exchanges, bankers to issue and their branches, underwriters and registrar to issue the date of filing of prospectus and schedule of opening and closing date of issue.

15. Distribution of Issue Materials

Issue materials such as prospectus, application forms, the brochures, posters and banners have to be distributed amongst the brokers, underwriters, bankers and investment centre at the various locations. The printers are responsible for the distribution of issue materials. The issuer in consultation with the merchant-bankers has to appoint or select printers. It will be convenient to the issuer and merchant-banker, if the printer has the necessary infrastructure facilities to effect delivery of the printed materials.

Based on the issue stationary requirements of the Stock Exchanges, SEBI, Registrar of Companies, Brokers, Underwriters, etc., the merchants banker decides the quantity of the issue materials namely prospectus, application forms, brochures, posters and bank schedules. After getting the ROC card the company places the order to the printer for prospectus printing. A draft application form with abridged prospectus has to be approved from the Regional Stock Exchange authorities before placing order for printing of public issue application forms. Lead Merchant-banker can finalise the distribution schedule and deliver copy to printer for delivery of issue materials to Bankers, Underwriters and Stock Exchanges. The new management functionaries are depicted in the Chart I.

Post-Issue Management Functions

The lead manager's work in the post-issue management has been considerably reduced. The major intermediary in the post-issue management is the registrar to the issue. From the date of opening of the subscription list for public issue till the despatch of the share certificate is completed, the registrar to the issue take over the work. But the lead manager is in a position to get co-operation from the registrar in connection with deciding the date of closure of the issue, submitting the 90 per cent minimum subscription report to SEBI and suggest the basis of allotment to the issuer.

1. Receipt of Collection of Reports

On the day or the next day the issue closes for public subscription, the stock exchange authorities all over India have to be intimated via telegram or fax message regarding the closing of the subscription list. In this connection, the lead merchant-banker suggests the date of closure of the issue to the issuer based on the level of subscription. For sending the report in time the lead manager meets collection reports. Therefore, the first job of a lead merchant-banker in post-issue activities of a public issue is to get collection details about the issue. The company in co-operation with the lead merchant-banker and registrar to the issue should follow up with the bankers to the issue for early collection of application forms, stock invest etc.

Apart from sending the intimation to share-stock exchange, it is obligatory on the part of the lead manager to file the 7 days report of 90 per cent minimum subscription

CHART I – New Issue Management Functionaries

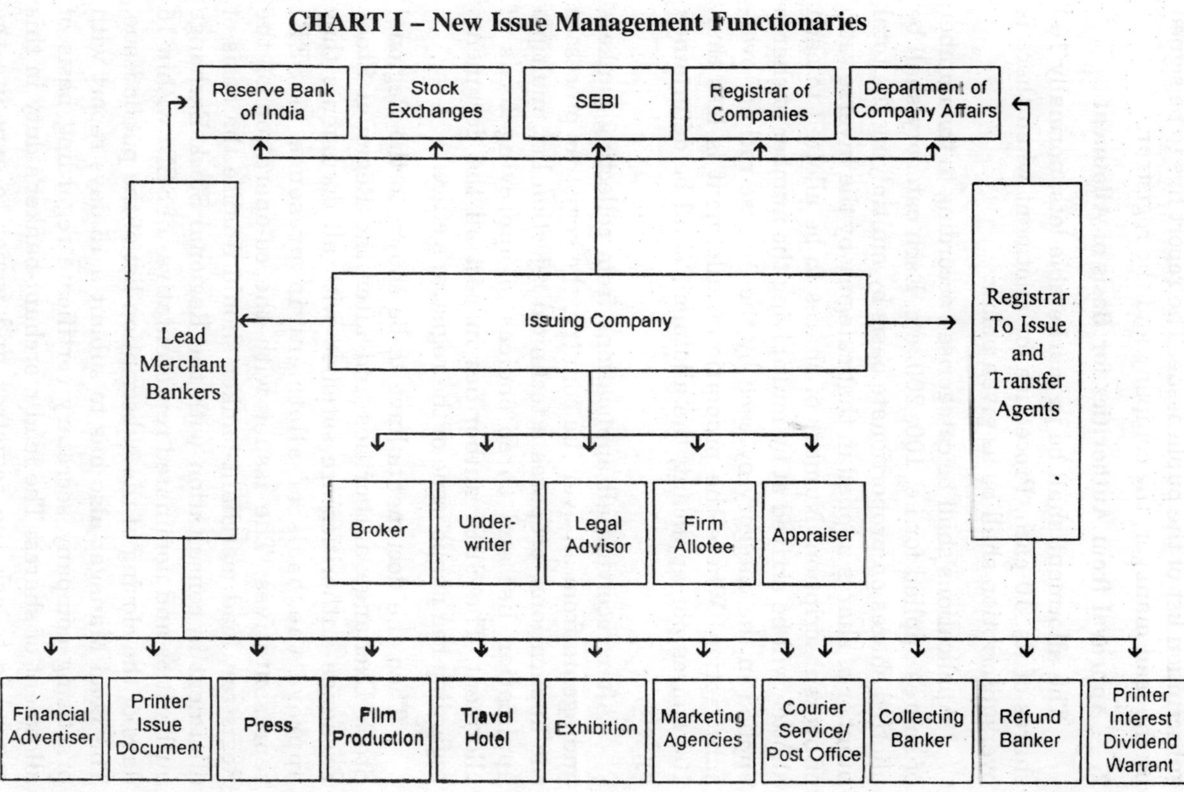

report with the SEBI within 7 days of the closing of the subscription list of the public issue. The report has to be signed by the lead manager, the company and the registrar.

2. Approval from Authorities for Basis of Allotment

The allotment shall be in marketable lots, normally 100 shares of Rs. 10 each. Procedure for allotment when there is oversubscription shall be as given below:

Applications shall be categorised according to the number of shares applied for i.e. 100, 200, etc. Each category shall be allotted shares on proportionate basis by multiplying the total number of shares applied in that category by the inverse ratio of oversubscription. Number of shares to be allotted to each allottee will be arrived at by multiplying the number of shares applied in the category by each by the inverse ratio of over-subscription. Where the proportional allotment is less than 100 shares per applicant, the allotment shall be determined by lots.

After receiving all applications from collecting bankers and agents from all over the country, the registrar processes the applications, prepares a technical rejection list, multiple application list and three choices of approving basis of allotment. The SEBI authorities inspect all the documents regarding the public issue of the registrar's office.

Then the documents have to be shown to the Regional Stock Exchange authorities and after the Regional Stock Exchange authorities are satisfied with all documents they approve the basis of allotment in presence of SEBI representatives. The issuer with the co-operation of the Registrar, lead merchant-banker should finalise the basis of allotment in consultation with the Regional Stock Exchange authorities and nominated representatives of SEBI within 15 days of the closing of the subscription list of the public issue. The Lead Manager also has to submit a 15 days report with practising company secretary certificate regarding basis of allotment of shares. The lead merchant-banker's duty in this regard is to ask the registrar and issuer to expedite the allotment work as per the guidelines of the capital issues.

3. Assistance in Sending Refund Order/Share Certificate

The required share certificates, allotment notices, refund orders are to be printed in advance and they have to be drafted by the lead merchant-banker as per direction of issuer. Then it is to be filed with the regional stock exchange for their due approval by the issuer.

The responsibilities of the lead manager ends only if the subscribers have received the share certificate or refund order. Hence, he must make follow up with issuer and registrar of the issue whether they send the refund order or share certificate to the subscribers or not.

4. Assistance in Listing Securities

Then the company files listing application with all its required enclosures, listing agreement, distributing schedules, auditor's certificate regarding cost of public issue, allotment of promoters quota shares and enforcement of promoters quota shares regarding lock-in-period etc., with listing fees etc. The listing application must be filed with the Stock Exchanges within 70 days from the closure of the subscription list. The stock exchanges on being satisfied with the documents and papers and being convinced that all share certificates, allotment advises, refund orders and underwriting commission cheques and brokerage cheques have been despatched within 70 days of the closing of the subscription list, permits the company for listing and trading of its shares on their exchanges. In this connection the lead merchant-banker has to arrange the various documents to be submitted to the authorities and pursue the company to list the shares as early as possible.

5. Assistance in Settlement of Claims

After the shares of the company are listed on the stock exchanges as promised in the prospectus the public issue job is almost over, leaving only the implementation part of the project to the promoters. It is the duty of the lead merchant-banker for making arrangement for paying brokerage, underwriting commission, printers and advertiser dues by the issue in time. The whole exercise of the lead merchant-bankers in the new issue management is depicted in the form of a process flow chart in Chart II.

CHART II – New Issue Management Process Flow Chart

PRE- ISSUE

Sources of Procurement
↓
Selection of the Issuer
↓
Agreement with Issuer
↓
Documentation
↓
Appraisal/Assistance for appraisal
↓
Arrangement of Project Finance
↓
Preparation of Due Diligence
↓
Vetting of Prospectus
↓
Appointment of Intermediaries
↓
Assistance to obtain consents/approvals
↓
Pricing the Issue
↓
Marketing Strategies
↓
Publicity Campaign
↓
Fixing Timing of Issue
↓
Distribution of Issue Materials

↓

POST-ISSUE

Receipt of Collection Reports
↓
Approval from authorities for basis of allotment
↓
Assistance in sending refund/certificate
↓
Assistance in listing
↓
Assistance in settlement of Claims

REFERENCES

1. Avadhani, V.A. *Investment Management*. Himalaya Publishing House, Bombay, 1996, pp. 327–328.
2. Sundanthiram S.S., "Marketing of Public Issue". *The Economics Times,* New Delhi, Ist August 1992, p. III.
3. "Policy and Documentation". *The Merchant Banker Update,* Jan. 1997, p. 61.

3

Merchant Bankers – General Profile

In India, the merchant banking activities are regulated by the Securities and Exchange Board of India (SEBI). According to Merchant-bankers rules, 1992 "Merchant-banker" means any person who is engaged in the business of issue management either by making arrangements regarding selling, buying or subscribing to securities as manager, consultant, advisor or rendering corporate advisory services in relation to such issue management. In the light of the above definition merchant-banker means one who undertakes the issue management and it is related function. The new issue management function is a highly specialised job and it is subject to high standard of performance. It is essential to have proper organisational structure in the merchant banking organisation. Hence, in this chapter the data collected about the merchant-bankers with regard to background information and organisation details have been taken up for discussion.

Year of Establishment

The years of establishment of the study units are presented in the Table 3.1. The year of commencement of business varied from 1904 to 1995. The private Merchant-bankers have started their business in two phases, namely 11 units from 1978 to 1987 and another 8 units from 1988 to 1997. One of the Private Sector Banks was established in the year 1904. It is the seasoned bank and it is going to celebrate the centenary within 6 years. Similarly one of the Nationalised Banks had started its business before 1977. It is important to note here that most of the units were conducting the merchant banking activity only from 1993 onwards. But they started their business before 1993 for the purpose of conducting banking or non–banking financial or stock broking or financial institutions.

Table 3.1: Year of Establishment

(N = 26)

Year	*Types of Merchant-bankers*						*Total*
	AFI	*SFI*	*NB*	*NBS*	*PSB*	*PMB*	
Before 1977	–	1	1	–	2	–	4
1978-1987	1	–	1	–	–	11	13
1988-1997	–	–	–	1	–	8	9
Total	1	1	2	1	2	19	26

Note: 1. AFI – All India Financial Institution
2. NB – Nationalised Banks
3. PSB – Private Sector Banks
4. SFI – State Financial Institution
5. NBS Nationalised Bank Subsidiary
6. PMB – Private Merchant-bankers

Registration with SEBI

The Securities and Exchange Board of India was set up as an administrative body in April 1988. From April 1990, onwards, any person or body corporate either engaged in or proposing to engage in the business of merchant banking is required to obtain prior authorisation of SEBI. SEBI was given statutory status on 30.1.92 by promulgation of SEBI Ordinance which has since become an Act of Parliament.

In the early Nineties, most of the Non-Banking Financial Companies switched over from leasing and hire purchasing business to pure issue management and underwriting business. "Easy norms made for easy entry into the Merchant banking business. With a minimum capital-base requirement of Rs. 1 crore and the perception that merchant banking meant only handling public issues, all and sundry jumped into the fray in 1991-92—that including manufacturing concerns."[1] Therefore, the real growth of merchant-bankers took place during the period 1992–93. Table 3.2 shows the Registration of Merchant-bankers with SEBI.

Table 3.2: Registration of Merchant-bankers with SEBI

Year	*Types of Merchant-bankers*						*Total*
	AFI	*SFI*	*NB*	*NBS*	*PSB*	*PMB*	
1990	–	–	1	–	–	–	1
1992	–	–	–	1	1	4	6
1993	–	1	1	–	1	10	13
1994	–	–	–	–	–	4	4
1995	–	–	–	–	–	1	1
1997	1	–	–	–	–	–	1
Total	1	1	2	1	2	19	26

It is evident from the above table during the year 1992–93 nineteen units obtained authorisation from the SEBI.

Communication Facilities

Merchant-bankers should have adequate amount of infrastructure facilities for getting the authorisation from SEBI. While granting the authorisation, SEBI takes into consideration not only the professional competence, capital adequacy, track record and experience but also the availability of infrastructure. These facilities will help to conduct the issue management activities more accurately and quickly. The SEBI criteria for authorisation of merchant-bankers stressed that the merchant-bankers should possess at least 2 computer terminals, adequate office space and manpower.

The infrastructure facilities particularly for information technology possessed by the study units are given in Table 3.3.

As evident from Table 3.3, all the Merchant-bankers were having the computers and printers. At the same time there were merchant-bankers who have more than 2 computers. Twenty-four Merchant-bankers were having the fax facilities. Eleven merchant-bankers were having the E–mail facilities.

Table 3.3: Communication Facilities

Equipment Name	*Types of Merchant-bankers*						*Total*
	AFI	*SFI*	*NB*	*NBS*	*PSB*	*PMB*	
Computer	1	1	2	1	2	19	26
Printer	1	1	2	1	2	19	26
Fax	1	1	2	1	2	17	24
E-Mail	1	1	–	–	1	8	11

Location of Merchant-bankers

Generally, there is much concentration of merchant banking activities in the western region of India with head offices of the merchant banking division/subsidiaries of banks and private merchant-bankers in Mumbai. The obvious reason for the development of this phenomenon is that the head-offices of most of the commercial banks and other financial institutions, playing crucial role in providing term-loans, underwriting and subscribing to the capital issues, are in Mumbai only. It facilitates the merchant banking banks/ companies to attend to various matters more expeditiously and promptly through personal contacts with the officials, who are in a position to take final decisions. Moreover, many mutual funds, foreign financial institutions and financial institution's head office are located in Mumbai. Hence the merchant-bankers wish to open either head office or at least branch office in Mumbai. Equally, places like Kolkata, Delhi, Chennai, Ahmedabad and Hyderabad have attracted the merchant-bankers to open their branch office because these places have chance to establish companies as well as more number of the investors situated and the premier stock exchanges are located in these places.

However, in the recent past, an increasing number of private merchant-bankers have come up in metros other than Mumbai, the financial capital of the country. Now it is the other regions than the western region which are picking up and hold good promise of industrial growth. The location of the branches of merchant-bankers are given in Table 3.4.

Table 3.4: Location of the Branches

Branches situated	*Types of Merchant-bankers* AFI	SFI	NB	NBS	PSB	PMB	*Total*
Mumbai	1	–	2	1	1	16	21
Delhi	1	1	1	1	2	8	14
Kolkata	1	–	–	1	1	6	9
Chennai	1	–	1	1	2	9	14
Hyderabad	–	–	–	–	–	6	6
Cochin	–	–	–	–	–	6	6
Ahmedabad	–	–	–	1	–	4	5
Bangalore	–	–	–	1	–	6	7
Other Places	–	2	–	1	–	24	27

Note: Other places includes the following: Jaipur 3, Coimbatore 3, Indore 3, Vijayawada 3, Pune 2, Thirvanandhapuram 2, Vadodra 2, Agra 1, Noida 1, Brailey 1, Thane 1, Salem 1, Vishakapattinam 1, Madurai 1, Nagpur 1, Bhopal 1.

It is evident from Table 3.4 that the sampled merchant-bankers were having their branch offices mainly in Mumbai but at the same time they were also having their branch offices in other places too.

Investor's Base of Merchant-bankers

The term Investor means a person or body corporate who undertakes to subscribe the shares or debentures of the company. Investor includes general public, Foreign Financial Institution, Financial Institutions, Mutual Fund Operators and Corporate Bodies. As per the SEBI's stipulation the Issuer is to have firm allotments as well as reservation for these categories of investors, the trend is to go for Pre-writing of the issue so that the risks of selling the issue are minimised. The strength of the Merchant-bankers is gauged by the ability to attract and keep the investors like the FIIs, FIs, MFs etc.

Hence the merchant-bankers should have the regularly sponsored investors in their books. This would facilitate the Pre-writing of the issue. This is an added advantage to the merchant-banker to grab the issue mandate from the proposed issuer company. Table 3.5 highlight the investor's base of the selected merchant-bankers.

Table 3.5: Investor's Base of Merchant-bankers

Investors	*Types of Merchant-bankers*						*Total*
	AFI	*SFI*	*NB*	*NBS*	*PSB*	*PMB*	
Foreign Financial Institutions	1	–	1	1	1	5	9
Financial Institutions	1	1	1	1	1	2	7
Mutual Funds	1	1	–	1	–	4	7
Public Investors	–	–	1	–	–	16	17
Corporate Bodies	1	1	1	1	1	14	19

It can be observed from table 3.5 that the Private Merchant-bankers were utilising all the investors and they relied more on the corproate bodies. The companies were investing their surplus money into the shares and debentures of the other companies. Further, the banks and financial institutions were having financial institution and foreign financial institution investors as their strength.

Membership in Stock Exchanges

As per, Ministry of Finance notification on 13th November, 1992, Corporate Bodies are allowed to become the member of a Stock Exchange. This would pave the way for the Merchant Banking companies to enter into the stock market operation. The smooth functioning of the secondary market operation will promote new issue market indirectly and give more business to the merchant-bankers. In another aspect, if the merchant-banker has the corporate membership in stock exchange, it not only gives revenue to merchant-banker but also facilitates to interact with broking community, strengthens the retail marketing and aware of the latest knowledge about the secondary market. This in turn helps the merchant-banker to decide the issue price and appraise the project efficiently. The details about the corporate membership in the stock exchanges by the select merchant-bankers are given in the Table 3.6.

Except the three study units, all the other merchants bankers were having the membership in the stock exchanges in different places. Some of the merchant-bankers had membership in stock exchanges in more than one places. Among the stock exchanges the OTCEI and NSE have attached more number of the study units. The reasons behind this increasing number of membership in these stock exchanges are (i) The fee for membership is relatively less, (ii) They are screen based exchanges and (iii) There is a country-wide-net work.

Table 3.6: Membership in Stock Exchanges

Place of Stock Exchanges	*Types of Merchant-bankers*						*Total*
	AFI	*SFI*	*NB*	*NBS*	*PSB*	*PMB*	
Mumbai	1	–	–	–	–	4	5
Delhi	–	–	–	–	–	1	1
Kolkata	–	–	–	–	–	1	1
Chennai	–	–	–	1	–	3	4
Hyderabad	–	–	1	–	1	3	5
Cochin	–	–	–	–	–	1	1
Coimbatore	–	–	–	–	–	2	2
NSE	1	–	–	1	–	7	9
OTCEI	–	1	1	1	–	12	15
None	–	–	1	–	1	1	3

Membership in SRO's

SEBI has been impressing upon all the players in the capital market to form their respective SROs (Self-Regulatory Organisation) for exercising discipline on their own. The merchant-bankers are not exempted from this. There are two associations working for the betterment of the merchant banking community. They are (i) Association of Merchant-bankers in India and (ii) All India Private Merchant-bankers Association.

The interested merchant-bankers have the membership in these two associations or any one of the associations. The sampled units which are having membership in these associations are presented in Table 3.7.

All the sampled units were not having the membership in the association. The four merchant-bankers have not enrolled as a member in any of the associations. Further, out of 26 study units, 20 units had membership in the AMBI. Only 2 units had membership in both of the associations. A few units were not having membership in any association.

Table 3.7: Membership in Association

Membership in Associations	*Types of Merchant-bankers*						*Total*
	AFI	*SFI*	*NB*	*NBS*	*PSB*	*PMB*	
AMBI	1	1	1	1	1	15	20
AIPMB	–	–	–	–	–	–	–
Both	–	–	–	–	–	2	2
None	–	–	1	–	1	2	4
Total	1	1	2	1	2	19	26

Brokers/Underwriters Network

The share brokers and sub-brokers have been playing an important role in public issues. The relationship between the merchant-bankers and brokers is crucial because brokers actually sell the issue in our present retail system of distribution and selling. Mr. R. Subramaniam, Assistant Vice President of Lloyds Finance says that "The Merchant-banker should have a good sub-broker network for the success of an issue or alternatively have the ability to underwrite."[2] Hence the success of an issue mainly depends on the performance of the broker, sub-broker and underwriter network. Table 3.8 explains how the sampled merchant-bankers are relied on the following supporting service for the success of the public issue.

It can be observed from Table 3.8 that out of the 26 merchant-bankers 4 of them fully depended on the brokers, another 3 depended on the sub-brokers and brokers, one merchant-banker relied on the sub-broker/underwriter and 9 relied on all of them. Further, 4 private merchant-bankers, 2 Nationalised banks, one private sector bank and one State Financial Corporation did not depend on the brokers/underwriter network. This might be due to the underwriting ability of the

Table 3.8: Brokers/Underwriters Network

Reliance on	*Types of Merchant Bankers*						*Total*
	AFI	*SFI*	*NB*	*NBS*	*PSB*	*PMB*	
Brokers	–	–	–	–	–	**4**	**4**
Brokers/Sub-Brokers	–	–	–	–	–	**3**	**3**
Brokers/ Underwriter	–	–	–	–	–	**1**	**1**
Sub-Brokers/ Underwriter	–	–	–	–	–	**1**	**1**
Broker/Sub-Broker/ Underwriter	**1**	–	–	**1**	**1**	**6**	**9**
None	–	**1**	**2**	–	**1**	**4**	**8**
Total	**1**	**1**	**2**	**1**	**2**	**19**	**26**

above stated organisations. It is concluded that all the sampled units necessarily depended on the services of the broker/sub–broker and underwriter for the success of the issue. The nationalised banks and private sector bank and state financial corporation did not depend on the brokers and sub–brokers or underwriters network for their new issue marketing.

Location of Brokers and Underwriters

The location of the brokers and underwriters spread to the width and breadth of the country. As one August 1995 there were 6000 brokers and 750 sub-brokers in our country.[3] A merchant-banker can choose any broker or sub-broker for the issue assignments. There is a practice among the merchant-bankers and issuers to offer an extra commission namely "kitty" to the brokers for securing of application money to a certain stipulated level. Hence, there is a clear understanding between the leading merchant-banker with the broker community. In general certain brokers and sub-brokers regularly undertake the issue business from the issuer through the particular merchant banker. Table 3.9 depicts the regular sponsor of broker, sub-broker and underwriter of issue and their locations.

Table 3.9: Location of Brokers and Underwriters

Location	*Types of Merchant-bankers*						*Total*
	AFI	*SFI*	*NB*	*NBS*	*PSB*	*PMB*	
Mumbai	1	–	–	1	1	12	15
Chennai	1	–	–	1	–	11	13
Delhi	1	–	–	1	–	3	5
Kolkata	1	–	–	–	–	3	4
Hyderabad	–	–	–	–	–	7	7
Cochin	–	–	–	–	1	1	2
Coimbatore	–	–	–	–	–	2	2
Ahmedabad	–	–	–	–	–	1	1
Lucknow	–	–	–	–	–	2	2
Vadodhra	–	–	–	–	–	1	1
Dehradun	–	–	–	–	–	1	1
None	–	1	2	–	1	4	8

Note: The Merchant-bankers who are not depending on a particular broker or sub-broker are unable to indicate their places.

It can be observed from Table 3.9 that the majority of the brokers/sub-brokers and underwriters were located at major cities namely Mumbai, Chennai, Delhi, Hyderabad. The reason behind this was the merchant banking head office or branch office were situated in those places. It was found to be convenient to the sampled merchant-bankers to carry on their campaigns more intensively in these cities.

Research Activities

The aim of conducting research is not only to improve the quality of the issue but also very helpful to acquire more business. Table 3.10 shows the research activities of the sample merchant-bankers.

Out of the total 26 merchant-bankers only 11 were conducting research. Among the 11, 8 were the private merchant-bankers and the remaining included All India Financial Institution, Nationalised bank and Nationalised bank subsidiary one each. But the merchant-bankers reported that they were utilising the data published by the Prime Database,

Table 3.10: Research Activities

Types of Research	Types of Merchant Bankers						Total
	AFI	SFI	NB	NBS	PSB	PMB	
Equity Analysis	–	–	–	–	–	4	4
Industry Analysis	1	–	1	–	–	3	5
Investment Analysis	–	–	–	1	–	1	2
None	–	1	1	–	2	11	15
Total	1	1	2	1	2	19	26

The Economic Times, Financial Express, The Hindu Business Line, Business World, Business India, Business Today, Capital Market, Dalal Street Journal and Centre for Monitoring the Economy (CMIE) with regard to the New Issue Management.

Function of Parent Body/Sister Concern

It is very essential that a merchant-banker should have good relations with as many intermediaries as possible. Such intermediaries would include advertising agencies, registrars to the issue, printers of stationery, brokers, fellow merchant-bankers, underwriters etc. But if the merchant-banker himself offers the other intermediary services it will immensely help the merchant-bankers. Because the merchant-banker need not depend on others, and it will be helpful to search additional income from the allied services. Mostly the nationalised banks and private banks are rendering these services as bankers to issue, collecting and refund banker services. This service gives an additional income to the merchant-banker and it is also an assured income if the merchant-banker is lead managing the issue. The details about the merchant-bankers' parent association and sister concern functioning as the intermediaries are given in Table 3.11.

It is observed from Table 3.11 that most of the private merchant-bankers' parent/sister concerns were acting as a non-banking financial companies. These non-banking companies' main business was the mobilisation of deposit. This provided money muscle to the merchant-banker. The success of the issue not only depended on the effective marketing of the issues

Table 3.11: Parent Body/Sister Concern Function

Functions	*Types of Merchant Bankers*						*Total*
	AFI	*SFI*	*NB*	*NBS*	*PSB*	*PMB*	
Issue Related							
Registrar	–	–	–	–	–	4	4
Banker to Issue	–	–	2	1	1	–	4
Advertiser	–	–	–	–	–	1	1
Refund Banker	–	–	1	–	1	–	2
Underwriter	–	–	–	1	–	6	7
Others							
Corporate Bodies	–	–	–	–	–	3	3
Stock Broking	–	–	–	–	–	4	4
Non Banking Finance Companies	–	–	–	–	–	16	16
Financial Institution	1	–	–	–	–	–	1
Nationalised Bank	–	–	2	1	–	–	3
Portfolio Manager	–	–	–	–	–	2	2
None	–	1	–	–	1	1	3
Total	1	1	5	3	3	37	50

but also on extending the underwriting of the issue, the term lending and syndication of loan facilities to the issuer. Apart from the private merchant-bankers the private sector banks and nationalised banks subsidiaries were functioning as refund bankers and collecting bankers.

Compliance Officer/Principal Officer

As per SEBI regulation of merchant banking, it is necessary on the part of a merchant-banker to identify an officer, who is responsible for interpreting various rules, regulations etc. and gives necessary advice to operating staff members to ensure strict compliance with regulatory requirements and performance in desired manner. This officer is known as Compliance Officer or Principal Officer. Those Merchant-bankers who are having large number of assignments should ordinarily have a full-time Compliance

Officer, others may have a part-time Compliance Officer for this purpose.

Generally, officers other than compliance officers are not expected to seek personal discussion with SEBI officials for seeking clarification of Regulations and Guidelines. Hence, it is desirable that the Merchant-bankers at least designate a senior board member or senior staff member as a full-time or part-time Compliance Officer. Mostly the Vice-President or managing director of the merchant banking division of the organisation may be designated as a Compliance Officer. Some of the merchant-bankers designate any one of the professionally qualified employees as a principal officer for their outfits. In the following pages the details of principal officer of the select Merchant-bankers are discussed.

Educational Background

In order to render various services to the entire satisfaction of the clients, the Merchant banking divisions of banks and Financial Institutions and Private Merchant banking companies have to employ an impressive team of experts in various fields of knowledge, particularly in financial management, corporate finance and accounts, and company law. These officers are highly qualified and experienced persons, with proper attitudes, capable of tactfully dealing with well-informed and experienced company executives, and convincing them of the merits of the point of view of the former. The teams include the company secretaries, MBAs, CAs, Cost Accountants etc., specialised in company law and secretarial practice, banking, cost accounting, corporate finance, and marketing etc. Sometimes even the engineering experts are appointed by the Merchant banking divisions/private merchant banking companies to advise on technical matters. The Merchant banking divisions of Nationalised banks as well as the Private Merchant banking companies are reported to be having as many as 4 to 18 expert executives looking after a number of specialised jobs pertaining to merchant banking. Table 3.12 states the educational qualification of the principal officers of the select Merchant-bankers under study.

Out of the 26 Merchant Banking outfits, 9 outfits' principal officers were having professional qualifications, 6 were having

Table 3.12: Educational Qualification of Principal Officer

Qualification	*Types of Merchant Bankers*						*Total*
	AFI	*SFI*	*NB*	*NBS*	*PSB*	*PMB*	
Under-graduate	–	–	–	–	1	1	2
Post-graduate	–	1	1	–	–	–	9
Professional	–	–	–	–	1	8	9
Post-Graduate and Professional	1	–	1	1	–	3	6
Total	1	1	2	1	2	19	26

post-graduation as well as professional qualifications. Fifteen merchant banking outfits' officers had the post graduate diplomas. Only two outfits' officers had the under-gaduation diplomas and they may be promoted as principal officer by their experience.

Designation of Principal Officer

The nomenclature of the principal officer varies from institution to institution. Some of them are called as Vice-President and others as General Managers. The different nomenclatures of the principal officer used by the Merchant-banker are described in Table 3.13.

It is inferred from Table 3.13 that the All India Financial Institution's principal officers were called as the Managing Director. The State Financial Institution's principal officer was called as General Manager and most of the private merchant-bankers used the designation of the principal officer as Vice-President or General Manager.

Age of the Principal Officer

In India, the merchant banking activity is of recent origin and it requires acumen, prophecy and vigil on the part of the principal employees. Hence, most of merchant banking companies invariably have on their staff, well-qualified young men with initiative and drive, on the assumption that they take the decision quickly and be willing to accept the

Table 3.13: Nomenclature of Principal Officer

Designation	*Types of Merchant Bankers*						*Total*
	AFI	*SFI*	*NB*	*NBS*	*PSB*	*PMB*	
Vice-President	–	–	–	–	–	7	7
Chairman	–	–	–	–	–	1	1
Managing Director	1	–	–	–	–	1	2
Director	–	–	–	–	–	2	2
Senior Executive	–	–	–	–	–	1	1
General Manager	–	1	–	–	–	4	5
Senior Manager	–	–	–	–	–	1	1
Chief Manager	–	–	–	–	1	–	1
Assistant General Manager	–	–	1	–	–	–	1
Assistant Manager	–	–	–	–	–	1	1
Manager	–	–	1	–	1	1	3
Senior Project Manager	–	–	–	1	–	–	1
Total	1	1	2	1	2	19	26

responsibilities voluntarily. Therefore, the officers of the merchant banking concerns are happened to be young and with lesser number of years of experience. Table 3.14 indicates the age group of the principal officers of the study units.

Table 3.14: Age Group of Principal Officer

Types of Merchant Bankers	*< 30*	*30-40*	*40-50*	*50-60*	*60 >*	*Total*
AFI	–	–	–	1	–	1
SFI	–	1	–	–	–	1
NB	–	1	1	–	–	2
NBS	1	–	–	–	–	1
PSB	–	1	1	–	–	2
PMB	2	8	9	–	–	19
Total	3	11	11	1	–	26

It is inferred from Table 3.14 that the age of principal officers of the sampled units was in the range between 30 to 50 years of the 26 merchant banking units, 11 officers were under the age group of 30 to 40 years. Another 11 officers came under the age group of 40 to 50 years. It may be concluded that majority of the principal officers of the sampled units were under the age group of 30 to 50 years and 14 merchant bankers' principal officers were in the age group of 30 to 40 years.

Experience of the Principal Officer

No doubt, the professional qualification of the principal officer can help to understand the issue management problems very quickly. But that alone will not make the issue management business a success. Therefore, there must be adequate amount of experience in the issue management business. The principal officer of a merchant bank is supposed to make sure that all the relevant information which have been supplied by the issuer for the disclosure in the prospectus, due diligence etc., are true and authentic. Very recently (10th December 1996), SEBI has decided not to vet the prospectus. In this case the responsibility of the lead managers is much larger than ever before. However, it is practically impossible to verify the authenticity of each and every piece of information disclosed in the prospectus. Mostly, the lead merchant-bankers usually rely on the management's declaration and the auditors' certificate. Naturally, this calls for good amount of experience. An experienced officer alone can know how to gather and verify the information from the issuer and which part of information is most relevant to the purpose and which type of information may be accepted as such from the issuer. Table 3.15 highlights the experience of the principal officer under study.

It is inferred from Table 3.15 that 10 out of 26 merchant banking outfits' principal officers were having less than 5 years experience. Another 10 outfits' principal officers had experience of 5 to 10 years. In other words, 20 merchant banking outfits' principal officers were having less than 10 years experience. This phenomenon may be due to the development of merchant banking business has taken place only after the enactment of the separate Ruels and Regulation for Merchant banking by

Table 3.15: Experience of Principal Officer

Years	*Types of Merchant Bankers*						*Total*
	AFI	*SFI*	*NB*	*NBS*	*PSB*	*PMB*	
Less than 5	–	–	–	1	1	8	10
5 to 10	–	1	2	–	1	6	10
10 to 15	1	–	–	–	–	5	6
Above 15	–	–	–	–	–	–	–
Total	1	1	2	1	2	19	26

the SEBI. Hence, it is natural that the majority of principal officers were having less than 10 years experience.

Salary of the Principal Officer

It is quite essential to appoint an experienced and technically qualified financial experts to run the merchant banking organisation. To fulfil the above purpose the merchant banking personnel has got to be paid quite high salaries, and the infrastructure facilities for running Merchant banking activities have necessarily to be of quite high standard. As the number of merchant banking outfits has been increased tremendously, to keep the qualified principal officer in tact within the organisation, the organisation should necessarily pay high amount of salary to principal officer. Table 3.16 gives the monthly salary details about the principal officer of the merchant-bankers under study.

Table 3.16: Salary of the Principal Officer

Monthly Salary	*Types of Merchant-bankers*						*Total*
	AFI	*SFI*	*NB*	*NBS*	*PSB*	*PMB*	
Less than 10000	–	–	–	–	–	1	1
10000 to 20000	–	1	2	1	1	14	19
20000 to 30000	–	–	–	–	–	4	4
30000 and above	1	–	–	–	1		2
Total	1	1	2	1	2	19	26

It can be understood from the Table 3.16 that 19 principal officers of the different merchant banking outfits were getting monthly salary ranging from Rs. 10,000 to Rs. 20,000. Another 6 principal officers got more than Rs. 20,000 as their monthly salary. Most of the private merchant-bankers' principal officer drew their salary ranging from Rs. 10,000 to Rs. 20,000.

Special Courses attended by the Principal Officer

In the banks/financial institutions, the officer selected for Merchant banking department/divisions were not only experienced in various aspects of commercial banking/finance functioning but also well-oriented and trained in Merchant Banking. Already certain short- and long-term courses are being organised and conducted by the Reserve Bank of India, UTI Capital Market and Research, Institute of Chartered Financial Analysis, Nationalised banks, Management Institutes, and the Institute for Financial Management and Research, Chennai for the benefit of the banks/financial institutions/non-banking financial companies running or planning for Merchant banking business. The principal officer's of the banks/financial institutions and private merchant banking outfits are attending these courses for the development of their career in merchant banking. The academic as well as practical knowledge are imparted in the training courses. Table 3.17 explains the special courses on merchant banking attended by the principal officers of the study units.

Table 3.17: Special Courses attended by the Principal Officer

Special Courses	*Types of Merchant-bankers*						*Total*
	AFI	*SFI*	*NB*	*NBS*	*PSB*	*PMB*	
Attended	1	1	1	–	–	6	9
Not Attended	–	–	1	1	2	13	17
Total	1	1	2	1	2	19	26

Table 3.17 clearly indicates that the 9 merchant banking outfits' principal officers alone have attended the special courses on merchant banking. Further, there were 17 principal officers who have not yet attended any special course on merchant

banking. Out of the 17, the private sector merchant banking outfits' principal officers constituted 13. The reasons for not attending the course may be due to the higher amount of course fees charged by the training institutions, lack of specialised staff in training institutions and inadequate infrastructure facilities.

Strength of the Employees

"To a large extent emphasis is placed on the size and reach of the merchant-banker. "Bigger the better" holds true in this business and particularly for the mega issues. Here the size means infrastructure availability, manpower, number of branches, sub-broker network and procurement capabilities."[4] Hence, the success of the merchant banking business requires adequate manpower sources as well apart from other requirements. An organisation's strength is based on the appropriate number of employees. The employees of an organisation are normally categorised into three namely managerial, supervisory and operative. The details about the average number of employees in each of these categories in the study units are given in Table 3.18.

Table 3.18: Employees Details
(Average Number of Employees)

Nature of Employees	*Types of Merchant-bankers*					
	AFI	*SFI*	*NB*	*NBS*	*PSB*	*PMB*
Managerial	4	2	2	3	4	2
Supervisory	5	6	2	5	4	2
Operative	10	7	3	6	3	3

Based on the data with regard to the employees, it is inferred that the some of the merchant banking outfits were having large number of operative staff members. The information about these two institutions included the total number of employees in all branches as well as head office. However, the nationalised banks, nationalised banks subsidiaries and state financial corporations were having lesser number of managerial staff members when compared to the other institutions. In case of operative staff, again the nationalised banks and private sector banks were having lesser number of the staff members. But most of the private merchant banking outfits had lesser number of employees in all three categories, when compared to the total work-load of the organisation. This may be due to the volume of issue management work undertaken by the study units and the administrative cost of holding the employees. To conclude the private merchant-bankers were running the merchant banking office with lesser number of employees.

REFERENCES

1. Swati Kamal and Sudeshne Sen, "Just Natural Selection", *The Economic Times,* 7th-13th February, 1997 p. 1.
2. Nandu Manjeswar, "Private Merchant-bankers flourish", *The Economic Times,* 24th April, 1994, p. 11.
3. A.B. Ravi et al., "New players in the Share Bazar". *Business India,* 14th-27th August, 1995, p. 64.
4. Ken source information services private limited, "Marketing the Mega Issues", *The Merchant-banker Update,* Jan. 1997, p. 27.

4

Analysis I—Pre-Issue Management

The issue management work starts with the mandate from the issuer. As and when the issuer submits the memorandum and articles of association and other relevant documents and information to the lead merchant-banker, the pre-issue management work commences.

The Lead manager activities in Issue management activities are broadly classified into two parts namely Pre-issue activities and Post-issue activities. The lead merchant-bankers enter into agreement to perform either pre-issue activity or post-issue activity or both. It depends upon the agreement between the issuer and the merchant-banker. Pre-issue management functions broadly include the following:

(i) Sources of procurement

(ii) Selection of Issuer

(iii) Pre-issue presentation

(iv) Agreement with issuer

(v) Preparational of project

(vi) Appraisal/Assistance for appraisal

(vii) Preparation of draft prospects

(viii) Preparation of due diligence

(ix) Assistance in appointment of Intermediaries

(x) Assistance to obtain consent/approval

(xi) Pricing the issue

(xii) Arrangement of project finance
(xiii) Marketing strategies
(xiv) Publicity campaign
(xv) Fixing the timing of the issue
(xvi) Distribution of issue materials.

Sources of Procurement

The merchant banking division of Nationalised banks and private merchant banking companies naturally depend first on their respective clients for rendering Merchant banking services. However, they cannot afford to confine their activities to their clients only, and a number of non-clients or new clients may be attracted. This is done through direct contacts with the ever-increasing number of prospective clients and intermediaries like underwriter, broker, advisor etc. For this purpose, most of the large merchant-bankers have a team of managers who are in constant touch with the prospective issuers and they develop a rapport with them. They get information about the prospective issuers through newspapers and business reports and sometimes from gossips. They also keep close touch with the firms and companies proposing to expand or modernise the industry and looking for the arrangement of long-term working capital. The

Table 4.1: Sources of Procurement of New Issue Business

Sources	*Types of Merchant-banker (Weighted Average Score)*						*Overall Weighted*
	AFI	*SFI*	*NB*	*NBS*	*PSB*	*PMB*	*Avg. Score*
Parent Body	8	7	7.5	8.0	6.5	2.68	3.920
Advisor	3	2	4.0	1.0	4.5	6.00	5.192
Clients	6	6	7.0	2.0	5.5	5.68	5.653
Underwriter	1	4	2.5	4.0	2.5	3.47	3.269
Auditor	2	3	1.0	3.0	2.5	4.21	3.650
Direct	7	8	6.0	7.0	7.5	6.95	7.500
Broker	5	5	4.5	5.0	4.0	3.95	4.115
Advertisement	4	1	3.5	6.0	3.0	2.42	2.692

parent organisation of the lead merchant-banker is also a good source of new issue business to Nationalised Banks and Financial Institutions and some of Private Merchant-bankers. It is quite natural that the merchant-banker may use one or more sources to acquire the new issue business. But the researcher wanted to know which source is preferred by them. Table 4.1 exhibits the various sources and their order of preference and the mean score.

It is clear from Table 4.1 that the major source to acquire new issue mandate was to approach the issuer directly as it had a overall weighted average score of 7.5. Another major source to acquire new issue business was the clients in other services and its relevant overall weighted average score was 5.65. It is understood that the clients who satisfied with other services of Merchant-bankers, entrusted the new issue business with the same merchant-bankers. This might be due to the variety of services rendered by the merchant-bankers to the clients.

Another source which influenced the merchant-banker to procure the issue mandate was the reference by company advisor or consultant. The advisor or consultant might be auditor, tax-consultant, corporate lawyer or finance expert. The advisor referred the merchant-banker's name to the issuer. The overall weighted average score for this factor was 5.19.

Hence it is concluded that the direct approach was the major source for acquiring issue mandate from the prospective issuer. Apart from this corporate clients, advisors were also having some influence on the merchant-banker in deciding for the proposed issue. Thus, the major source of new issue business was the direct access to the market. The other sources were clients and advisor.

Selection of Issuer

(a) Requirements for Selection of Issuer

With more and more companies planning to tap the capital markets, it has become imperative that the merchant-bankers should find good companies to their investors. Because the investors have now started rejecting new issues being promoted by a merchant-banker who has been associated early with the so-called dubious companies. Hence, before accepting a mandate from the companies the merchant-banker should check the company's past performance, background of promoters, the management pattern etc. Apart from these, the merchant-banker should first insist statutory conditions prescribed by the SEBI and by may also insist on certain pre-conditions of its own before accepting the issue mandate from the companies. The pre-condition of the sampled merchant-bankers before accepting the issue mandate are given in Table 4.2.

Table 4.2: Criteria in Selection of Issuer

Criteria	*Types of Merchant-bankers*						*Total*
	AFI	*SFI*	*NB*	*NBS*	*PSB*	*PMB*	
Statutory:							
Name in predominant place	1	1	2	1	2	15	22
Projects appraised by Banks/ Financial Institutions	1	1	2	1	2	16	23
Others:							
The size of the issue	–	1	–	–	–	2	3
Handling only bond issue	–	1	–	–	–	1	2
Handing only a specific industry	1	1	2	1	–	3	8
Handling only sound project	–	–	1	–	–	3	4
Parent/Sister Concern as one of the Supporting service organisations	1	–	2	1	2	5	11

It is obvious from the above Table 4.2 that some of the private merchant-bankers did not bother about the statutory criteria for accepting the issue proposal. In respect of the other condition, 11 merchant-bankers imposed a condition that their parent or sister concern would be one of the supporting service organisations namely registrar to issue, banker to issue, refund banker, advisor etc. This was because not only the merchant-banker but also the parent/sister concern would earn income and promote the business of the parent concern. It is to note that only four merchant-bankers had insisted that they handled only sound projects.

(b) Issuer's Demand

As stiff competition is prevailing in the market, the issuers select the merchant-banker who accepts their demands. The issuer may make many demands to the merchant-banker before entering into an agreement with the lead merchant-banker. Generally the issuer makes many demands to the private merchant-banker and private sector bank, as they lack money power and project finance. But these facilities are provided by the financial institutions and nationalised banks and therefore they attract the issuer. Table 4.3 lists the usual demands which were imposed by the issuer before entering into an agreement with the merchant-banker and the relevant mean score of them.

Table 4.3: Issuer's Demand

Demand	*Types of Merchant-banker (Weighted Average Score)*						*Overall Weighted*
	AFI	*SFI*	*NB*	*NBS*	*PSB*	*PMB*	*Avg. Score*
Promoter's Stake	1	2	4.5	5.0	5.5	5.05	4.76
Minimum No. of Shareholder	6	3	6.0	6.0	7.0	5.0	5.23
Bridge Loans	8	7	6.0	8.0	7.0	4.16	4.92
Project Finance	5	8	8.0	4.0	5.0	5.32	5.54
Over Subscription	2	6	2.5	3.0	3.5	4.47	4.15
Competition with in a Period	3	5	1.5	2.0	1.0	4.58	3.92
At Minimum Cost	7	4	4.5	7.0	4.5	5.63	5.50
Managing Somehow	4	1	3.0	1.0	2.5	1.79	1.96

Based on the opinion of the merchant-bankers under study and the overall weighed average score for the factors, it is concluded that most of the issuers demanded that the arrangement of project finance as their first and foremost demand. The overall weighted average score for this factor was 5.54. Another important (overall weighted average score 5.50) factor was issue at minimum cost. The third important demand of the issuer to merchant-banker was minimum of five shareholders subscribing Rs. one lakh each, which secured overall weighted average score of 5.23. Therefore, the issuer primarily insisted on three important aspects namely, merchant-bankers should make arrangement of project finance, manage the issue at a minimum cost and arrange to subscribe

5 shareholders for one lakh rupees each, to the merchant-banker. If the issuer's requirements were not fulfilled by the Merchant-banker, then he did not select the issuer.

(c) Selection of Industry

Merchant banking activity is a specialised activity. As there is severe competition prevailing in the new issue business, it is difficult to procure new issue mandate from the issuer. To procure new issue mandate, specialisation of a particular industry is of some importance apart from the infrastructure, manpower resources and marketing ability. Therefore the merchant-bankers want to differentiate from other merchant-banker in this line, by concentrating on a particular industry. The concentration of industry of the study units are given in Table 4.4.

Table 4.4: Selection of Industries

Selection	*Types of Merchant-bankers*						*Total*
	AFI	*SFI*	*NB*	*NBS*	*PSB*	*PMB*	
All industries	–	–	–	–	2	16	18
Specific industries	1	1	2	1	–	3	8
Total	1	1	2	1	2	19	26

It is evident from Table 4.4 that the Nationalised Bank and Financial Institutions were concentrating only on specific industries namely power, port, road and export oriented industries. The Nationalised Bank's subsidiary and some private merchant-bankers were also concentrating on specific industries other than finance companies, real estate, oil extraction and software development industries' projects. The rest of the private merchant-bankers and private sector banks were accepting new issue proposal from all types of industries. Because excepting a few, all other private merchant-bankers are conducted lesser number of new issue business. Therefore, they might constrained to accept whatever proposal comes to their way. It may be concluded that there was no concentration on particular line of industries in the case of private merchant-bankers and there was no specialisation and selection in their new issue business activities.

Agreement with Issuer

Before entering into an agreement with the issuer, the merchant-banker decides the charges for the issue management. The lead Merchant-banker's fees ranged between 0.50 per cent to 2.00 per cent of the issue price. The fee is negotiated by the merchant-banker with the issuer. It is mentioned in the offer documents. There is an assumption on the part of the merchant-bankers that they are rendering service without charges. To verify this, the researcher has studied the prospectus of 148 companies which deal with issues between January 1996 and June 1996, of the issues handled by the sample Merchant-bankers. Madras Stock Exchange has become helpful in this respect. Out of 148 prospectus studied, 35 prospectus of companies did not disclose the manager fee. Other 113 lead merchant-bankers fees varied and given in Table 4.5.

Table 4.5: Lead Merchant-banker Fees (% to Issue Size)

Range of fees	*Types of Merchant-bankers*						*No. of Companies*	*%*
	AFI	*SFI*	*NB*	*NBS*	*PSB*	*PMB*		
Below 0.50%	–	–	–	–	–	16	16	11
0.50% to 1.00%	3	1	1	3	–	59	67	45
1.00% to 2.00%	–	–	1	2	–	25	28	19
Above 2.00%	–	–	–	–	–	02	02	1
No Fees	–	–	1	2	–	32	35	24
Total	3	1	3	7	–	134	148	100

Source: Comped from the prospectus of Companies which made public Issue between January 1996 to June 1996.

Table 4.5 reveals that fifty-six per cent of the lead merchant-banker charged fees below 1.00% of the issue price. It is evident from the study that 35 out of 148 category 1 merchant-banker did not get any fees for their service. In this regard it is worthwhile to mention the following statement. "A Survey of all the 1,316 public issues, excluding mutual fund offers, in the financial year 1994-95 reveals that many merchant-bankers reached some "Special understanding" with the issuers before they took on the responsibility as merchant-bankers foı their issues. During 1994-95, as many as 413 recognised merchant-bankers of all categories were involved in marketing 1,316 public issues. But, only 70 merchant-bankers charged a fee for all their assignments."[1] Even though the present study is minuscule but there was some agreement with the survey results.

Therefore, the lead manager might not be very particular to lead managing fees. If lead manager foregoes fees he might be able to get income in other sources like acting as underwriter, collecting banker, refund banker, broker, registrar to issue etc., provided that the merchant-banker himself or his parent body or sister concern was performing other services.

Documentation

(a) Frequency of visit

The merchant-banker is supposed to gather a lot of information about the issuer's company for the documentation purpose. In this respect he should visit the issuer's office or project site to gather the information. Some of the seasoned merchant-bankers before accepting the issue mandate want to see, that the actual project linked with manufacturing concern or company premises if it is the non-manufacturing concern. Table 4.6 reveals the opinion about the frequency of visit made by the merchant-bankers under study.

Table 4.6: Frequency of Visit

Types of Merchant Bankers	*Number of Times*			*Total*
	Two	*Three*	*Four and above*	
AFI	–	–	1	1
SFI	–	1	–	1
NB	1	1	–	2
NBS	–	–	1	1
PSB	1	–	1	2
PMB	9	4	6	19
Total	11	6	9	26

Out of 26, eleven merchant-bankers twice visited the issuer company, 6 visited 3 times and remaining 9 made more than 4 times visit to the proposed project. The merchant-bankers are supposed to make more number of visits to issuer plant/premises to prepare the project thoroughly. If the merchant-banker visits the proposed project site or plant more number of times, it may help to avoid the dubious issue. But 9 sampled units alone made more number of visits to the issuer project location or premises.

(b) Number of Days for Documentation

The documentation work consumes much time of the merchant-banker. The major task in documentation is to collect the huge quantum of information regarding the project, promoter, financial data, documents details etc. The speed of the collection of information and completion of the work depend on the issuer, because he is going to supply the necessary information as and when required by the merchant-banker. If the issuer makes delay in providing the information, the merchant-banker will take much time to complete the pre–issue work. Therefore, the researcher wanted to know how many days are needed for the merchant-bankers to complete the documentation work. The respondents suggested the number of days needed to complete the documentation work. It is given in Table 4.7.

Table 4.7: Number of Days for Documentation

Duration	*Types of Merchant-bankers*						*Total*
	AFI	*SFI*	*NB*	*NBS*	*PSB*	*PMB*	
Less than 10 days	–	–	–	–	1	1	2
10 to 20 days	–	1	–	–	–	1	2
20 to 30 days	–	–	–	–	–	1	1
30 to 40 days	1	–	1	1	1	2	6
40 to 50 days	–	–	–	–	–	7	7
50 to 60 days	–	–	1	–	–	–	1
More than 60 days	–	–	–	–	–	3	3
Depends on Cases	–	–	–	–	–	4	4
Total	1	1	2	1	2	19	26

It is thus concluded that 13 out of 26 respondents felt that they needed 30 to 50 days for the documentation activities.

The above span of time required to complete the documentation activities thoroughly. But 8 out of 26 respondents felt that they needed more than 50 days, which was due to volume of information expected from the issuer.

Preference for Appraising Agencies

The recent (1996) SEBI's guidelines make appraisal compulsory. Banks/Financial Institutions are only allowed to appraise the projects and they should also subscribe at least 5 per cent of the issue price. Therefore, the Merchant-bankers are in a position to take up assignments of appraised projects. The appraisals build up credibility about the merchant-banker as well as the issuer in the minds of the investors. Further, as the appraiser of the project and/or term lenders is considered to be a positive inducement for accepting assignment by the merchant-banker. Therefore, it is worthwhile to know which institution's appraisals are most welcomed by the merchant-bankers under study. Table 4.8 exhibits the preference of the merchant-bankers with regard to the appraisal of the project.

Table 4.8: Preference for Appraising Agencies

Appraising Agencies	*Merchant-banker Group*						*Total*
	AFI	*SFI*	*NB*	*NBS*	*PSB*	*PMB*	
Financial Institutions	1	1	2	1	1	12	18
Banks	–	–	–	–	1	–	1
Both	–	–	–	–	–	7	7
Total	1	1	2	1	2	19	26

It can be observed from the Table 4.8 that 18 sample units preferred to get the project appraised from the Financial Institutions. Next to that appraisal of the project by both Financial institutions and Banks was preferred.

The main reason is, that if the project is appraised by these institutions the merchant-banker can arrange syndication of term loan easily for the issuer. The investors will have confidence to subscribe the issuer's company share, as the projects are thoroughly checked before granting loan to the issuer. However, among the study units, the Private Sector bank and SFI preferred appraisal of the project by their own institutions.

Arrangement of Project Finance

"To-day, Public issues are without public. For example, 86 per cent of the issues in 1995-96 could attract less than 5000 applicants each from across the country".[2] Therefore, the bulk of the issues have to survive through pre-arranged fund instead of general investor support. This further leads to strategic alliances between the promoters, issue financiers and merchant-bankers. "The promoter agrees to buy back from the financier the shares that are allotted to him at as much as 30 to 36 per cent over the listed price of the scrip".[3] Hence, the merchant-bankers have to arrange the financier on behalf of promoter for the success of the issue. Some of the merchant-bankers are themselves providing money through different route to the issuer for the success of the public issue. It is evident from the SEBI's inspection report that "Merchant-bankers were found to be involved in arranging syndication of funds towards promoters' contributions with a facility to buy back. An amount of one per cent of finance amount was charged as the syndication fee by merchant-bankers it is learnt".[4] Further it is almost common knowledge that the Banks and Financial Institutions' merchant-bankers, due to their financial power, term-lending relationships with the corporate clients, monopoly status in issue appraisal and equity stake in the appraised projects, are in a position to persuade or attract the

Table 4.9: Arrangement of Project Finance

Types of Merchant Bankes	*Agree*	*Undecided*	*Disagree*
AFI	1	–	–
SFI	–	1	–
NB	1	1	–
NBS	1	–	–
PSB	2	–	–
PMB	12	2	5
Total (%)	17 (65)	4 (15)	5 (20)

Note: Figures in parenthesis indicate percentage.

promoters to award the issue mandates to them or their subsidiaries. "Many issues were floated by finance companies—the response to which was questionable as quite a few were either financed or subscribed through one arrangement or the other".[5] The opinion of study units, regarding whether the arrangement of project finance is necessary for the success of the issue or not is presented in Table 4.9.

It is crystal clear that sixty-five per cent of the respondents were agreed that the arrangement of the project finance was essential for the success of the issue.

Due Diligence Certificate

(a) Disclosure of Information by Issuer

The submission of due diligence certificate by the merchant-bankers to the SEBI is a legal obligation. In this certificate, the lead merchant-bankers have to give an undertaking that they have examined various documents and other information connected with filing of the draft prospectus.

The merchant-banker relies on the information given by the issuer that can be used for preparation of the due diligence certificate. The merchant-bankers are supposed to gather information at their best efforts in spite of the fact that some of the issuers conceal the material facts. Therefore, the researcher elicited information in this regard from the sample merchant-bankers and presented in Table 4.10.

Table 4.10: Disclosure of Information by Issuer

Types of Merchant-bankers	*Agree*	*Undecided*	*Degree*
AFI	–	1	–
SFI	–	1	–
NB	1	1	–
NBS	–	1	–
PSB	1	1	–
PMB	11	7	1
Total	13	12	1
(%)	(50)	(46)	(4)

Table 4.10 clearly shows that 50 per cent of the respondents have agreed that the issuers not disclosed all information and reserved certain vital facts. It was very difficult for the merchant-bankers to have access to the necessary source to get the valid information for preference of due diligence certificate.

(b) Difficult to get information at ROCs

Another major difficulty faced by the merchant-banker is the information sought by the SEBI is not available to merchant-bankers through the issuer. Often merchant-bankers complain that the SEBI wants a phenomenal amount of information, all backed by supporting documentation, and such detailed information not always available in a country where information collection and processing are still in its infancy. One critical area on which SEBI wants information is market potential. "There are many industries for which detailed and reliable studies on market potential are not available. Information in any case is hard to come in India. And Planning Commission projections in various industries have often been proved wrong."[6]

Apart from registering and monitoring the company, the Registrar of Companies (ROCs) is an important source of corporate information for both investors and corporate bodies. The merchant-bankers have to gather necessary information from the company for the preparation of due diligence certificate. Sometimes the merchant-banker may not depend on the issuer information. He may ascertain whether the information given by the issuer is genuine or not. For all these practical purposes, the merchant-bankers depend on the ROC. Whether it is a copy of the annual report or the nature of the change created on the assets of a company, the investing public/ merchant-banker can look to ROC for financial information on corporate entities.

"A study states that as on March 31, 1995 there were 353,292 companies registered under the Companies Act. In Maharashtra alone, there are as many as 77,560 companies. Their affairs are monitored by two offices located in Mumbai, with a total staff strength of not more than 200. There is no way this level of manpower can effectively deal with problems of management of information flow and still promptly respond to queries from the public.[7]" Whether there is any difficulty in getting information at ROC's office is ascertained through the questionnaire. The relevant information is presented in Table 4.11.

Table 4.11: Difficult to get information at ROCs

Types of Merchant-banker	*Agree*	*Undecided*	*Disagree*
AFI	1	–	–
SFI	–	–	1
NB	2	–	–
NBS	1	–	–
PSB	1	1	–
PMB	13	2	4
Total (%)	18 (69)	3 (12)	5 (19)

Table 4.11 emphasises that the majority of the respondents (69 per cent) felt that there was some difficulty in getting the information in the ORC's office. This may be due to the inadequate infrastructure facilities and under–staff in the offices of the ROC in the different regions. Therefore, there is an urgent need to improve the staff and infrastructure facilities in the ROC's offices of all the regions. Here it is relevant to mention that, "The Working Group which went into the functioning of the offices of the ROC felt its offices are not adequately equipped. As a matter of fact, it went to the extent of recommending a one time investment of at least Rs. 60 crore to purchase and maintain the necessary equipment and related facilities."[8]

Activities that consume more time

The activities like documentation, preparation of draft prospectus, diligence and appraisal are consuming more time and energy of the merchant-banker. The merchant-bankers risk lie in these activities. Table 4.12 explains which type of work consume more time in pre-issue management.

Table 4.12: Activities that Consume More Time

Type of Activity	Types of Merchant Bankers						Total
	AFI	SFI	NB	NBS	PSB	PMB	
Documentation	–	1	–	–	–	7	8
Project Appraisal	–	–	–	–	1	3	4
Draft Prospectus	1	–	1	1	1	4	8
Due Diligence	–	–	1	–	–	5	6
Total	1	1	2	1	2	19	26

Nearly one-third of the merchant-bankers opined that the documentation consumed much time. Another 8 merchant-bankers felt that the preparation of the draft prospectus consumed much time. The documentation as well as the draft prospectus are hectic tasks to the merchant-banker. Because if he commits any mistake in this stage he will face serious problems later on. Therefore, the preparation of draft prospectus takes much time of the merchant-bankers, in the case of the management of pre-issue activities.

Vetting of Prospectus

The eligible issuer can make public issue without vetting a prospectus by SEBI or to obtain an acknowledgement card from SEBI. In other words, the merchant-bankers are allowed

Table 4.13: Vetting of Prospectus by Lead Manaers

Types of Merchant Bankers	Very Useful	Of Average Use	Not Useful
AFI	1	–	–
SFI	–	–	1
NB	–	2	–
NBS	–	1	–
PSB	2	–	–
PMB	13	2	4
Total (%)	16 (62)	5 (19)	5 (19)

to vet the prospectus of the issuer. Whether this decision of the SEBI is welcomed by the sampled merchant-bankers or not is the question. Table 4.13 below emphatically explains the views of the merchant-bankers in this respect.

Only 19 per cent of merchant-bankers opined that the vetting of the prospectus by merchant-bankers was not of much use. The right of vetting of prospectus to merchant-bankers was indirectly imposing the larger responsibilities to the merchant-bankers. But 62 per cent of units held the view that this particular function was absolutely essential for the issue process.

Further, it is interesting to note the reason stopping vetting of offer documents for public issues by SEBI. The SEBI Chairman D.R. Mehta says "That is the kind of system that exists in the developed markets. For example, in U.S.A. the offer documents are submitted to the Securities Exchange Commission (SEC). If the SEC has any observations, these are duly conveyed to the merchant-banker. We are following the same system now."[9] The merchant-bankers opinions about this empowerment to vet the new issue proposal of the clients are presented in Table 4.14.

Table 4.14: Rationale behind Vetting of Prospectus

Types of Merchant Bankers	*Better Transparency (A)*	*Escaping Responsibilities (B)*	*Creating More Business (C)*	*A+B+C*	*No Response*	*Total*
AFI	–	–	1	–	–	1
SFI	1	–	–	–	–	1
NB	–	1	–	–	1	2
NBS	1	–	–	–	–	1
PSB	2	–	–	–	–	2
PMB	11	3	3	2	–	19
Total	15	4	4	2	1	26

Of the 26 merchant-bankers, 15 study units revealed that the rationale behind in vetting of prospectus was to better transparency. Majority of the sample respondents disclosed that vetting of prospectus would result in better transparency of document.

Selection of Intermediaries

The Merchant-bankers have influence in selection of registrar/other intermediaries and help the issuing company to finalise the terms and conditions of appointment. Before recommending anybody as an intermediary to the issuer the merchant-banker should consider the following. "Quicker adoption of new technology (infrastructure) in information processing, streamlined and time bound adherence to schedules (Commitment) by other intermediaries and efficient (Quality) postal services will be key factors contributing to the good performance by registrars to the issue."[10]

If the issuer makes wrong choice of intermediary, later both the issuer and merchant-banker will face many problems. Some of the problems are:

(i) delay in getting the refund orders/money,

(ii) delay in getting share allotment letters,

(iii) the wrong entry in the share documents,

(iv) delay in despatch of forms, letters, etc.,

(v) delay in procurement of business,

(vi) development of issues,

(vii) difficulty in execution of time schedule etc.

Therefore, the merchant-bankers normally influence the issuer to fix up the intermediary of their choice. The researcher wanted to ascertain whether the merchant-bankers really influenced the issuer at the time of selection of the intermediary or not. If it was so, what were the reasons for the merchant-bankers to influence the issuer for selection of registrar. For this purpose, researcher elicited relevant information through the questionnaire and presented in Table 4.15.

It is found that only 4 out of 26 admitted that they were not interfering in the right of issuer to select the intermediary. Rest of the respondents have accepted that they influenced the issuer to select the intermediary on various reasons. Therefore, there is strong influence on the part of the merchant-bankers to decide the intermediary for the issue. The reasons for their influence is given in Table 4.15.

Table 4.15: Reasons for Selection of Intermediaries

Types of	*No*	*Influence and Reasons*									
MBs	*Influence*	*A*	*B*	*C*	*D*	*A+B*	*A+C*	*B+C*	*A+B+C*	*A+B+C+D*	*Total*
AFI	–	–	–	–	–	–	1	–	–	–	1
SFI	–	1	–	–	–	–	–	–	–	–	1
NB	1	1	–	–	–	–	–	–	–	–	2
NBS	–	–	–	–	–	–	1	–	–	–	1
PSB	–	1	–	1	–	–	–	–	–	–	2
PMB	3	6	–	2	–	1	–	1	5	1	19
Total	4	9	–	3	–	1	2	1	5	1	26

Note: A = Quality B = Infrastructures C = Commitment
D = Competitive Cost

Nine out of 26 merchant-bankers felt that they influenced the issuer to select the intermediary based on the quality of the work done on the previous occasion. Commitment is another important reason given by the three merchant-bankers for their influence.

Consent and Approval

(a) Approvals from SEBI

There are delays in the issuing of acknowledgement card by the SEBI. It is because of the sheer volume of the issues that came to SEBI, and SEBI official's do over-work. This is due to inadequate staff strength in the SEBI. For instance, SEBI has two dozen officers involved in surveillance, investigation and prosecution compared to a large contingent of over 1000 in the Security Exchange Commission (SEC) in USA.[11] A relevant question was put to the sampled merchant-bankers to ascertain, whether there is any delay in issuing the acknowledgement card by the SEBI. The opinion of the merchant-bankers is given in Table 4.16.

From the Table 4.16 it is evident that 22 (84%) out of 26 merchant-bankers agreed that there was delay in issuing the

Table 4.16: Delay in Approvals from SEBI

Types of Merchant-bankers	*Agree*	*Undecided*	*Disagree*
AFI	1	–	–
SFI	1	–	–
NB	1	–	1
NBS	1	–	–
PSB	2	–	–
PMB	16	2	1
Total	22	2	2
(%)	(84)	(8)	(8)

acknowledgement card and observation letter by SEBI. This was one of the reasons for giving the vetting right to the merchant-bankers by the SEBI.

(b) Approvals from Registrar of Companies

The issuer's very important duty is to submit the duly signed prospectus along with the enclosures to the Registrar of Companies and obtain the acknowledgement of filed in prospectus from the Registrar of Companies. It is a compulsory legal requirement. When the number of issues is more, the Registrar of Companies have heaps of prospectus for approval. But as in other Government offices, there is a serious

Table 4.17: Delay in Approvals from Registrar of Companies

Types of Merchant-bankers	*Agree*	*Undecided*	*Disagree*
AFI	1	–	–
SFI	–	1	–
NB	–	2	–
NBS	–	–	1
PSB	–	–	2
PMB	7	5	7
Total	8	8	10
(%)	(31)	(31)	(38)

infrastructure constraints, bureaucracy in the office of Registrar of Companies also. Hence, the researcher wanted to know whether the merchant-bankers are facing any difficulty in getting the acknowledgement card from the ROC's office. The information obtained from the merchant-bankers in this study is presented in Table 4.17.

It is inferred from the Table 4.17 that 8 respondents (31%) agreed that there was delay in ROC's office in clearance in public issue. At the same time 10 (38%) out of 26 expressed their view that there was no delay in the ROC's office. But 8 (31%) respondents remained undecided.

Pricing the Issues

(a) Preference in Pricing

There is a general impression that the manufacturing sector issues are priced much below the market price. But today, there is no control on pricing the issues. With certain regulatory mechanism the issuer and merchant-banker are free to fix up price according to the market trend. It may be below or above the market price or on par with it. It depends on the issuer's demand, strength of the projects, market sentiment and so on. But the sample merchant-bankers opined that they fixed up the price of issue on all the three levels and it depends upon the market conditions, investors' level of acceptance and the market price of the company's share etc. Table 4.18 explains the preference of the merchant-banker while pricing the issues.

Table 4.18: Preference in Pricing

Price Level	*Types of Merchant-bankers*						*Total*
	AFI	*SFI*	*NB*	*NBS*	*PSB*	*PMB*	
Above Market Price	1	–	–	–	1	6	8
Equal to Market Price	–	–	–	–	1	3	4
Below Market Price	–	1	2	1	–	10	14
Total	1	1	2	1	2	19	26

Of the 26 merchant-bankers, 14 expressed that they preferred fixing the issue price below the market price. Four have indicated that they preferred to fix up the price equal to the market price and remaining 8 expressed that they preferred to price them above the market price. At present the primary market is sluggish, and it compels the merchant-bankers to fix up the issue price either equal to or below market price to attract the investors.

(b) Fixation of Premium Amount

Almost all the existing company promoters who start the new enterprises are willing to mobilise funds through public issue of shares at premium. The premium collected through the public issue gives a lot of benefits to the issuer. The important few are:

(i) It reduces the issue cost.

(ii) It creates surplus and in turn it increases the borrowing powers.

(iii) It provides an in-built safety to the issuer to write off preliminary expenses.

The researchers has identified certain factors that are normally considered by the merchant-bankers and placed before the respondents to rank their preference of the factors in fixing the premium of the issue. Table 4.19 explains the factors as well as the preference of the merchant-banker in it. It also exhibits the overall weighted average score.

Apart from the above factors which are influencing the fixation of premium amount, there are some other factors which have influence. These factors were disclosed by the private merchant-bankers during the course of the interview. They are: Issue size, post issue equity, debt equity ratio, current market price and regulatory authorities guidelines etc.

It is evident from Table 4.19 that the promoters track record and fundamentals of the company were two important criteria to fix up the premium on the issue price. These two factors scored maximum overall weighted average score namely 9.81, 8.38.

Another important factor which influenced the pricing decision of the merchant-banker is the industry type. This factor secured overall weighted average score of 7.27. Certain

Table 4.19: Factors Influencing Premium

Factors	*Types of Merchant-banker (Weighted Average Score)*						*Overall Weighted*
	AFI	*SFI*	*NB*	*NBS*	*PSB*	*PMB*	*Avg.* Score
Promoters Track Record	9	11	11.0	7.0	7.5	10.5	9.81
Industry Type	11	10	7.0	11.0	8.0	6.68	7.27
Earnings Per share	8	8	8.5	6.0	6.5	7.10	7.19
Fundamentals	6	9	9.0	8.0	6.0	8.68	8.38
Market Standing	4	5	5.5	4.0	7.0	5.68	5.35
Project Nature	3	4	5.5	3.0	5.5	6.47	5.96
Market Sentiment	5	7	9.0	10.0	5.0	6.47	6.65
CCI Formula	1	1	3.0	1.0	2.5	4.05	3.50
Investors Preference	2	3	3.0	2.0	5.5	4.74	4.38
Issuer Compulsion	7	2	3.5	5.0	6.5	3.53	3.88
Instrument Type	10	6	1.0	9.0	6.0	2.89	3.62

industry public issues were conventionally priced at premium. In that case, the issuer was not in a position to fix up the share price at par or lower premium amount. The earning per share was yet another important factor while deciding issue price of the share. Its overall weighted average score was 7.19. Hence, it is concluded that no single factor was responsible to fix up the premium of the share. It was the combination of so many factors. Based on the data of our study, promoters track record, fundamentals of the company, industry type and earning per share are the four important factors which had influence on the fixing up of the premium on the shares.

Marketing Strategies

(a) Brokers and Underwriters Support

No doubt, the merchant-banker is a vital intermediary in the new issue management. But his efforts are materialised only with the help of the broker and underwriter. The brokers are the very essential intermediary in the new issue management. Without the help of the broker, the issuer does not procure the share application. There are some practical difficulties faced by the lead managers with regard to the broker and underwriter. In this regard the researcher wanted to ascertain the problems which are faced by the merchant-bankers while getting services from brokers and underwriters in new issues operations.

Table 4.20: Brokers and Underwriters Support

Types of Merchant Bankers	*Marketing Support*		*Procurement Ability*	
	Adequate	*Inadequate*	*Adequate*	*Inadequate*
AFI	–	1	–	1
SFI	–	1	–	1
NB	1	1	–	2
NBS	–	1	–	1
PSB	1	1	–	2
PMB	8	11	6	13
Total (%)	10 (38)	16 (62)	6 (23)	20 (77)

It is inferred from the Table 4.20 that the majority (62%) of the respondents were under the impression that the brokers' marketing support was inadequate in the marketing of the new issue. Again 77 per cent of the respondents opined that the brokers had the low level of procurement ability. There was a mismatch between the target and actual procurement.

(b) Firm and Preferential Allotment

Before 1993, listing in a stock exchange by a company was to offer 60 per cent of the securities to the public through prospectus. However, Rule, 19(2)(b) of the Securities Contracts (Regulation) Rules was amended on September 20th, 1993 reducing the percentage of public offer from 60 per cent to 25 per cent. At the same time SEBI has introduced the firm and preferential allotment system to the new issue market. The participants of the firm and preferential allotment scheme is the Foreign Institutional Investors (FIIs), Financial Institutions (FIs), Mutual Fund Operators, Non-Residents Indian (NRIs), Promoter's company employees, employees of the own company. (Refer the percentage of allotment to each category in the Annexure XIII). If firm allottee's withdraws

Table 4.21: Firm and Preferential Allotment

Types of Merchant Bankers	*Very Useful*	*Of Average Use*	*Not Useful*
AFI	1	–	–
SFI	–	1	–
NB	1	1	–
NBS	1	–	–
PSB	2	–	–
PMB	14	2	3
Total	19	4	3
(%)	(73)	(15)	(12)

partly or fully the offer made to him after filing the prospectus to the Registrar of Companies, then such portion should be taken up by the promoters. In the case of firm allotment to the employees of the company, no single employee shall be allotted in excess of 200 shares of Rs. 10 each. There will be no lock-in-period for firm allotment and the shares are freely transferable. Reservations to different categories shall be on competitive basis. Under this new system of preferential allotment," "the proportion of allotments to mutual funds and Financial Institutions has gone up from 3 per cent in 1992-93 to 20 per cent in 1993-94 and 60 per cent in 1994-95".[12] Hence, it is anybody's curiosity to find out the impact of the firm allotment and preferential allotment on the new issue management. The impact of firm allotment and preferential allotment in public issue is ascertained through the relevant question to the sampled merchant-bankers. Their views are demonstrated in Table 4.21.

It clearly shows that majority of the respondents (73%) agreed that the firm allotment and preferential allotment were basic for the success of the new issue and it would promote the new issue business.

(c) Safety Net

Safety net schemes have come up mainly because of the depressed sentiment in the Capital market. The small companies' issues cannot be marketed these days merely by giving incentives or heavy advertising. Instead, innovative schemes are being drafted which attract the investors. It is called a safety net. Under safety net scheme, the merchant-bankers agree to take over the shares at a specified price and specified number after the 6 months of the closure of the issue if the issue price is below the par value. In the Ballapur Industries, Gujarat Soaps and Transgene Bio Tech cases, the buy back offer price was at par with the issue price of the issue. But one of the sampled units of our study which lead manage the Vijay Solvent Ltd. issue, has made a commitment to buy back equity shares for Rs. 55 each till 6 months from the date of dispatch of shares to the investors. However, the issue price of the share is Rs. 40. Already a few merchant-bankers have introduced this safety net arrangement for the success of the issue. Whether this safety net scheme will really improve the investor confidence or not is a question. Because after introducing this particular scheme in the new issue process, only a handful of merchant-bankers are experiencing it. Hence, the opinion about this scheme is gathered from the study units and presented in the form of a Table 4.22 below.

Table 4.22: Usefulness of Safety Net

Types of Merchant Bankers	*Very Useful*	*Of Average Use*	*Not Useful*
AFI	1	–	–
SFI	1	–	–
NB	2	–	–
NBS	1	–	–
PSB	2	–	–
PMB	15	–	4
Total	22	–	4
(%)	(85)	–	(15)

Eighty-five per cent of the respondents held the view that the safety net scheme was definitely improving the new issue market. But most of the merchant-bankers have practised buy back arrangement unofficially with the lenders and financier and not with the investors.

Publicity Campaign

The new issue advertisement may be released in two ways namely advertisement through print media or electronic media. The choice of media depends on so many factors such as nature of the issue, size of the issue, cost and time etc. Electronic media usually is preferred by the issuer who makes the mega issue. But there is no hard and fast rule in the choice of the media. It all depends on the timing of the issue, issues preference. The researcher inquired about the choice of media of the sample merchant-bankers under study. Their views are expressed in Table 4.23 below.

Table 4.23: Choice of Media

Types of Merchant Banks	*Print*	*Electronic*	*Both*
AFI	–	–	1
SFI	–	–	1
NB	1	1	–
NBS	–	–	1
PFB	1	1	–
PMB	15	4	–
Total	17	6	3
(%)	(65)	(23)	(12)

Out of the 26 merchant-bankers 17(65%), preferred to select the print media for their new issue advertisement. Most of the private sector merchant-bankers pr ferred the print media, because their size of the issue was ormally small. The AFI, SFI and NBS preferred both the print and electronic media as their size of the issue was normally big. Twenty three per cent (6) of the merchant-bankers selected the electronic media for new issue advertisement.

Fixing Timing of the Issue

(a) One Year Validity Period for Public Issue

Earlier, the acknowledgement card issued by SEBI was valid for a period of three months. From 14th May 1997 onwards, the observation letter issued by SEBI will have a validity of one year i.e. the issue opening date shall be within 365 days from the date of the observation letter is issued. In cases where no observation letter is issued, the period of 365 days shall be reckoned from the 22nd day of filling the draft other document with SEBI. The SEBI has considered the down sliding primary market condition and it is very difficult for the issuer to mobilise the funds from the primary market within the stipulated time. Another reason is "in 1995-96, according to the Primary Market Monitor, 334 of the 1428 public issues (including debt) that opened for subscription could not close on the earliest closing date."[13] Many issuers are making postponement of their issue due to the sluggish primary market condition. This can be avoided by merchant-banker who has some more time to decide the appropriate issue date based on the market condition. Therefore, it gives long time to the issuer and merchant-banker for making the public issue. The impact of the above guideliens are put to the merchant-bankers under study. Their opinions are demonstrated in Table 4.24.

Table 4.24: One Year Validity Period

Merchant-banker Group	*Very Useful*	*Of Average Use*	*Not Useful*
AFI	1	–	–
SFI	1	–	–
NB	1	–	1
NBS	–	1	–
PSB	1	1	–
PMB	11	3	5
Total	15	5	6
(%)	(58)	(19)	(23)

Six out of 26 23 per cent respondents only felt that the above decision of the SEBI would not be useful. But the 77 per cent (58 + 19) of the respondents felt that the decision of the SEBI was definitely giving a breathing time to both the issuer and merchant-bankers.

(b) *Timing of the Issue*

The decision taken by the issuer and merchant-banker about the timing of the issue is almost 45 days before the issue and there is no chance to make changes once the issue open date is decided. As a result, the decision is taken not only based on present market conditions but also on the anticipated market conditions after 45 days. Hence, there always exists a great degree of uncertainty about the success of the issue. Therefore, deciding the issue open date is a crucial aspect in the new issue management work. If an issue is floated in unsuitable time, it may miserably fail to catch the investors. There are many reasons which influence fixation of a particular date. It is to be noted that not even a single factor may influence the fixing opening date for an issue. Many factors are considered at the same time and the issuer acceptance is also very important in fixing up the opening date of an issue.

The researcher, has identified certain factors which are responsible for fixing the issue open date and asked the respondents to specify their preference in fixing the date of opening of the issue. The results are exhibited in Table 4.25.

Table 4.25: Timing of the Issue

Factors	*Types of Merchant-banker (Weighted Average Score)*						*Overall Weighted*
	AFI	*SFI*	*NB*	*NBS*	*PSB*	*PMB*	*Avg. Score*
Market Trend	10	10	9.0	10.0	10.0	9.16	9.307
Investors Psychology	1	2	9.0	4.0	5.5	8.11	7.307
Forthcoming No. of issues	8	5	7.0	8.0	9.0	7.95	7.846
No. of Mega Issues	6	6	5.0	7.0	7.5	6.79	6.650
High Market Price	2	9	3.0	3.0	4.5	4.26	4.230
Issuer's demand	9	3	4.5	9.0	7.5	6.05	6.153
Fourthcoming Budget	4	7	4.0	5.0	3.0	4.05	4.115
Sebi's Expiry Time	7	4	5.0	6.0	4.5	4.0	4.307
Auspicious Day	3	1	3.0	1.0	2.5	2.16	2.192
Favourable Stock Exchange Index	5	8	5.5	2.0	1.0	2.47	2.884

The market trend (9.307) was the most important factor in fixing the timing of issue. Apart from the market trend the reasons like investor's psychology (7.307), forthcoming number of issues (7.846) and number of mega issues (6.650) on the card were also having equal bearing on the decision of the timing of the issue. SEBI acknowledgement card expiry time also had equal footing on the decision of the timing of the issue.

(c) Time-lag Between Issue Open Date and Acknowledgement Card Date

The time is the most crucial aspect in the marketing of the issue. Mostly it depends on the general sentiments of the stock market. In the normal course, the timing is the essence of any marketing strategy. However, in Indian conditions one may not have the flexibility of waiting for favourable stock market conditions to launch an issue since the permission from the SEBI and other authorities may expire. For this purpose the researcher studied prospectus of 148 companies which made public issue during January 1996 to June 1996. The time-lag between issue open date and acknowledgment card date was studied by scrutinising those 148 prospectus of different companies which were handled by sample merchant-bankers. The results are given in Table 4.26 below.

Table 4.26: Time-lag between issue and acknowledgement card date

No. of days	*Types of Merchant-bankers*						*Total*
	AFI	*SFI*	*NB*	*NBS*	*PSB*	*PMB*	
30–59	1	–	1	2	–	33	37
60–89	–	–	–	2	–	41	43
90–119	1	–	–	2	–	22	25
120–149	–	1	1	–	–	16	18
150–179	1	–	1	1	–	14	17
Above 180	–	–	–	–	–	8	8
Total	3	1	3	7	–	134	148

Source: Compiled from the Prospectus of the Companies which made Public Issue between January 1996 to June 1996

Table 4.26 reveals that in majority of the cases the time lag was for a period of 30 to 89 days spell from the issue open date to acknowledgement card date. The issuer can fix up the issue date after getting the acknowledgement card. Two companies issue open date were 293 and 365 days respectively from the acknowledgement card date.

Distribution of Issue Materials

The printers are responsible for the distribution of issue materials such as prospectus, application forms, brochures, posters and banners. These issue materials should be distributed to brokers, underwriters, bankers to issue, investment centre, stock exchanges, etc. in time. If they do not reach in time to various intermediaries, the success of the issue will be affected. Therefore, the printer should plan the distribution method well in advance and he should follow the time schedule strictly. The researcher wanted to ascertain from sample merchant-bankers whether the printer follows the time schedule strictly or not. In this aspect, the necessary information has been gathered and presented in Table 4.27.

Table 4.27: Distribution of Issue Materials

Types of Merchant-bankers	*In time*	*Not in time*
AFI	1	–
SFI	–	1
NB	1	1
NBS	–	1
PSB	1	1
PMB	5	14
Total (%)	8 (31)	18 (69)

It is thus concluded that 69 per cent of the respondents felt that printers did not strictly follow the time schedule. There was some delay in reaching the issue materials to various intermediaries.

REFERENCES

1. V.S. Fernando, "Service for a fee or free service." *The Merchant-banker Update,* October, 1995, p. 29.
2. Prithivi Haldiea, "Another Feeble Attempt". *The Economic Times,* 18th November 1996, p. x.
3. Calcutta Bureau, "SIDBI Plans Refinance for Market Making in New Issues" *The Economic Times,* 25th Feb. 1996, p. 1.

4. Rajeswari Adappa Thakur, "SEBI finds lapses in due diligence". *The Economic Times,* 8th May, 1997 p. 9.
5. Rishi Roop Tripath, "Rewind 96-Public issues". *The Economics Times,* 1st Jan. 1997, p. 7.
6. Rajiv Shirali. "Capital Issues Prospectus go public". *The Economic Times,* 1st March, 1992, p. 14.
7. D. Sampathkumar, "ROCs—running last in the information race". *The Hindu Business Line,* 16th March, 1997 p. 7.
8. *Ibid.,* p. 7.
9. Shirish Natkarni, "We do require additional powers", *The Merchant Banker Update,* April, 1997 pp. 9-10.
10. Krishna Kumar Agarwal, *"New Issue Market Operation in India",* Kanishka Publishers, Distributors, New Delhi, 1997, p. 152.
11. Thusar Pania and Vinod Kumar, "Is SEBI doing enough". Business India. 21st September to 4th October, 1998, p. 62.
12. J.N. Kapur. "The State of Primary Market". *The Merchant-banker Update,* September, 1995, p. 15.
13. Vivek Bhargava, "The Colour of Money is Red". *The Economic-times* (Corporate Dossier), 22nd-28th November, 1996, p. 1.

5

Analysis II—Post-Issue Management

The post-issue activities are generally comprising of the following activities: (1) Receipt of Collection Report, (2) Submission of mandatory report to Stock Exchanges and SEBI, (3) Obtaining approval from stock Exchanges and Registrar of Companies, (4) Finalisation of basis of allotment, (5) Assistance in sending refund order or share certificate, (6) Assistance in listing securities, and (7) Assistance in Settlement of Dues. In ordinary course the shares or debentures are allotted in consultation with the issuer and registrar to the issue. But in the case of over-subscription, it is allotted in consultation with Issuer, Registrar, SEBI, Stock Exchange and Public representatives.

The merchant-banker may advice the registrar and issuer to make arrangement for refund of money for unallotted shares, payment of Brokerage to brokers, commission to underwriters, sending share certificate to the allottee's and stock exchange listing. These functions are examined in detail in the following paragraphs.

Receipt of Collection Report

(a) Consumption of Time

Under the existing system, the application forms along with cheques are deposited by investors in the various branches of banks designated as collection centres. Apart from having to communicate collection figures every day, branches have to process application forms, prepare schedules and reconcile them with the cheques cleared. After the process of reconciliation is complete, the branches issue a certificate, giving the final tally with details. The difficulty here is the process itself and it takes more than 30 days. There are further delays as the stock exchanges approve the basis of allotment only on receipt of final certificate by the controlling branch of each bank. During the course of personal discussion with the merchant-bankers, they opined that there are delays because banks are just not geared to meet the administrative demands on them. Further, the unions opposing computerisation and the large volume of applications putting increasing load on the banks, they are severely constrained. Table 5.1 reveals that the opinion of the sampled merchant-bankers with regard to the getting of collection report from the Banker to the Issue.

Table 5.1: Consumption of Time

Types of Merchant-bankers	*Agree*	*Undecided*	*Disagree*
AFI	–	1	–
SFI	1	–	–
NB	1	1	–
NBS	1	–	–
PSB	1	–	1
PMB	13	1	5
Total	17	3	6
(%)	(66)	(11)	(23)

Seventeen out of 26, (66%) agreed that it took much to the collecting banker to send the collection report to the issue. Yet another strong complaint against bankers to issue, from merchant-bankers was that the delay was particularly high in the month of March. "There is, however, little motivation to speed up the administrative process." Agrees A.P. Rao, managing director, Canbank Financial Services.[1] Because banks enjoy a short-term deposit as companies are not allowed to use the funds till the allotment is completed.

(b) Adequacy of Information

The researcher wanted to know whether the collection report received by the lead merchant-banker from registrar/

bankers to issue is adequate or not. Hence, the relevant information is gathered from the respondents and it is presented in Table 5.2.

Table 5.2: Adequacy of Information

Types of MBs	*Adequate*	*Inadequate*
AFI	1	–
SFI	–	1
NB	1	1
NBS	1	–
PSB	1	1
PMB	6	13
Total	10	16
(%)	(38)	(62)

Sixteen out of 26 (62%) merchant-bankers agreed that the report received from the banker to issue was inadequate. During the personal discussion with the lead merchant-bankers, they opined that the staff of the bankers' did not pay much attention to the report preparation work, because they considered that it was an extra work to them.

(c) Collection after Official Closure

There is not only delay in sending the collection reports to the registrar or issuer but also delay in the reconciliation of the accounts. The bankers to the issue delay due to certain benefits. First is the commission at the rate of 0.125 per cent of application money collected. Second is the brokerage on procurement of application money. Third is the short term deposit i.e. float money. Hence, there is a strong incentive for banks to continue accepting application forms for days after the official closure of an issue. Even in some branches, the counter accepting the application money for which the banker is not designated as the banker to issue. The researcher wanted to know whether the collecting-banker accepts the new issue applications, after the intimation of the lead manager/ issuer to stop the collection of applications, money. In this connection necessary information is gathered through questionnaire. The result is presented in Table 5.3.

Table 5.3: Collection after Official Closure

Types of MBs	*Agree*	*Undecided*	*Disagree*
AFI	–	1	–
SFI	–	1	–
NB	1	–	1
NBS	–	–	1
PSB	1	–	1
PMB	14	1	4
Total	16	3	7
(%)	(62)	(11)	(27)

As found in Table 5.3 it is evident that 62 per cent of the respondents have agreed that the bankers to the issue collect the application money after the closure of the issue. During the personal discussion with the lead merchant-bankers they opined that issuer plead the banker to collect the application money after the closure of the issue for the success of the issue.

(d) Reconciled Account Statement

The delay in closure of the issue, cause further delay in the reconciliation of the accounts. Therefore, the researcher wanted to ascertain whether there was a delay in sending the reconciled accounts statements by the banker to the issuer or registrar. Table 5.4 shows the opinion of the merchant-bankers in this regard.

Table 5.4: Delay in Reconciled Account Statement

Types of MBs	*Agree*	*Undecided*	*Disagree*
AFI	–	1	–
SFI	1	–	–
NB	1	1	–
NBS	–	1	–
PSB	–	1	1
PMB	16	1	2
Total	18	5	3
(%)	(69)	(19)	(12)

As found in Table 5.4 it is concluded that nearly 69 per cent of the respondents have agreed that the Bankers to the issue took much time to reconcile the accounts.

Approval for Allotment

(a) Finalisation of Allotment

The Bombay Stock Exchange and other stock exchanges have amended their listing requirements in accordance with the SEBI guidelines. The amendment is that a company has to make allotments to the public within 30 days of the closure of the public issue and pay interest at the rate of 15 per cent p.a. in case of delay in despatching refund orders. The earlier stipulation was that a company has to make allotments to the public within 70 days of the closure of the public issue. This particular stipulation gives a lot of workload to the issuer, registrar and merchant-banker. Even when 70 days were allowed, many registrars were unable to complete the allotment and send the refund orders to the investors in time. But now the time allowed is very limited and within a short span of 30 days, the registrar has to get the approval from the stock exchange and get the collection report from the banker to issue. The merchant-bankers also have the responsibility to see to it whether the investors received the allotment letters or refund orders in time. Hence, the researcher asked the merchant-bankers to express their opinion about this issue. The opinion of the sampled merchant-bankers are given in Table 5.5.

Table 5.5: Allotment Within 30 days

Types of MBs	*Very Useful*	*Of Average Use*	*Not Useful*
AFI	1	–	–
SFI	1	–	–
NB	2	–	–
NBS	1	–	–
PSB	2	–	–
PMB	14	1	4
Total	21	1	4
(%)	(81)	(4)	(15)

Out of 26 respondents, 21 (85%) have firmly agreed that it was absolutely essential and very useful, as it would speed up the allotment work and it enables investors to get allotment of shares or refund orders very shortly. This will further improve the new issue business. The not allotted investors may invest their money into some other new issues.

(b) Consultation for Allotment

As soon as the shares are allotted and refund orders are sent to the investors, the job of the merchant-banker is over. But in the case of registrar to issue, his job is not over in some cases. They are allowed to act as transfer agents to the issuer. This is a long time relationship with the issuer. Hence, it is everybody's guess that the registrar is more lenient to the issuer and they may not be accommodative and consultative with the merchant-bankers. There is a general report among the merchant-bankers that the registrars to issue are not interested in consulting the merchant-bankers and they resort to some irregularity with the issuer. There are clear evidences of a number of cases in which the registrars are not consulting the merchant-bankers. To quote: "Vrushi Financial Services had made allotments on faulty or incomplete share applications, while the more deserving investors were turned down. Rams Financial Services was debarred for returning the surplus money of an oversubscribed issue through ordinary mail instead of the prescribed registered post."[2] The SEBI has discovered that "there is irregular allotment practices in the case of public issues of over 25 companies. These companies could face suspension from trading in the stock exchanges where they are listed."[3] Table 5.6 indicates the opinion of the sampled merchant-bankers in this regard.

Most of the merchant-bankers (69%) disagreed that the registrar to the issue was not consultative with the merchant-bankers. Only 19% of the respondents agreed that the registrar was not consultative with the merchant-bankers. It is assumed that the merchant-bankers are having close connection with the registrars and if any irregularity takes place in the issue process, it is well within the knowledge of the merchant-bankers.

Table 5.6: Issuer Consult Before Allotment

Types of MBs	*Agree*	*Undecided*	*Disagree*
AFI	–	–	1
SFI	1	–	–
NB	1	1	–
NBS	–	–	1
PSB	1	–	1
PMB	2	2	15
Total	5	3	18
(%)	(19)	(12)	(69)

(c) Promoter's Influence in Allotment

"In an investigation into the functioning of nearly 10 leading registrars based at Delhi, Bombay and Calcutta, SEBI has discovered that share applications meant for public subscription were diverted to the promoters quota in a few cases. Also employees' quota of shares were offered to non-employees, many of them were wives and children of bank employees and other government officials."[4] The above observation of the SEBI has given interest to gather information whether the registrars allot the shares as per the guidelines of the SEBI or is it based on the promoter's will and pleasure. Table 5.7 explains the involvement of promoters in the allotment of shares by the registrars.

Table 5.7: Promoter's Influence in Allotment

Types of MBs	*Agree*	*Undecided*	*Disagree*
AFI	–	1	–
SFI	–	1	–
NB	–	1	1
NBS	–	–	1
PSB	–	–	2
PMB	1	6	12
Total	1	9	16
(%)	(4)	(35)	(61)

Surprisingly, most of the merchant-bankers (61%) disagreed that the registrars did not allot shares on the promoter's will and they confirm that the registrar followed the SEBI's guidelines and consulted the merchant-bankers in the allotment of shares.

(d) Infrastructure Facilities of Registrar

Share registration has become more extracting and technically intensive with the growth of the equity market. But the norms relating to functioning as a Registrar have not been updated. Big firms like Karvy Consultants Private Limited, SRG Financial, PCS Industries Limited, AMI–Computers Limited, Online Share Management and Cameo Share Registry Limited etc. have upgraded facilities.[5] In the case of others they continue to enrol as Registrars by merely fulfilling the minimum requirements of a 600-sq-feet office and 10 computer terminals. It is worthwhile to ask the merchant-bankers whether the registrar has adequate infrastructure facilities or not. Table 5.8 gives an interesting picture about the status of the infrastructure facilities of the registrar.

Table 5.8: Infrastructure Facilities of Registrar

Types of Merchant-Bankers	*Agree*	*Undecided*	*Disagree*
AFI	1	–	–
SFI	1	–	–
NB	1	1	–
NBS	1	–	–
PSB	–	2	–
PMB	15	3	1
Total (%)	19 (73)	6 (23)	1 (4)

It is clearly evident from Table 5.8 that the registrars had inadequate infrastructure facilities. Almost 73% of the respondents felt that the registrars were not having adequate infrastructure and technical upgradation.

Assistance in Sending Allotment and Refund Orders

In the event of share allotments, both the lead manager and the registrar shall be held responsible for any irregularity detected in the allotments. As per the new practice, an official of the lead manager along with a public representative shall monitor the allotments. A registrar has to face action when it goes up to de-authorisation in case of detection of serious irregularities whereas the merchant bank could get penalty points for the same. Hence, it is the primary concern of the merchant-banker to see to it, whether the shares are allotted by the issuer with the help of the registrar as suggested by him or not. Generally, registrars have been blamed for the extremely slow procedure involved in sending the allotment letters, refund orders and transfer of shares. As per latest (1996) stipulation of Stock Exchange, the issuer may allot the shares within 30 days. Now, the responsibility on the part of the registrar and the merchant-banker are more and they have to finish the allotment work very quickly. The speediness of the allotment work entirely rests with the registrar of the issue. If the registrar does the allotment work slowly it hampers the goodwill of the merchant-banker as well as the issuer. Perhaps, the reduction of number of days in allotment (from 70 days to 30 days) is mainly because SEBI has received a number of complaints from the investors. So, the researcher wants to ascertain whether the registrar to the issue performs the allotment work up to the expectation of the merchant-banker or not. In this regard, the following information (Table 5.9) is gathered from the study units.

Table 5.9: Distribution of Allotment and Refund Orders

Types of Merchant-bankers	*Agree*	*Undecided*	*Disagree*
AFI	–	1	–
SFI	1	–	–
NB	2	–	–
NBS	–	1	–
PSB	–	1	1
PMB	4	3	13
Total	7	6	13
(%)	(27)	(23)	(50)

It is concluded from Table 5.9 that only 7 (27%) out of 26 respondents were agreeing that the registrar made delays in the allotment and refund. But 13 out of 26 (50%) were disagreeing that the registrar did the allotment and refund orders work in a delayed manner. This may be due to the right selection of the registrar by the merchant-bankers, because the merchant-bankers have influence in the selection of the registrar.

Assistance in Listing of Securities

(a) Number of Listing

There is a grace among the issuers to list their shares in the premier stock exchanges. Among the premier stock exchanges they are very much concerned about listing in the Bombay stock exchange. Whether he is small company promoter or blue-chip company promoter the natural choice is to list the shares in Bombay stock exchange. But out of the 7500 (1997) listed shares in the Bombay stock exchange hardly 150 are regularly traded and another 1500 shares are frequently traded. This results in poor performance. The Bombay stock exchange delisted the companies which are not submitting the half-yearly annual reports or renewing the listing fees etc. Hence, it is essential to restrict the issuer to list their shares in too many exchanges. In another way it is better to list first in the regional stock exchanges and list one or two based on the issue size of the company. It gives more business not only to the regional stock exchanges but also there is a possibility of trading shares in the regional stock exchanges. In this connection it is worthwhile to mention the report of the Society for Capital Market Research and Development. The study says that, "Companies belonging to a particular region have a stronger attraction for investors residing in the same region compared to 'out side' companies. The physical proximity of investors to a company's office or to its manufacturing facilities both exercise some regional pull and should be taken into account in the marketing of new issues".[6]

Table 5.10 emphasises that 89% of the respondents agreed that the number of listing should be based on the issue size. This will reduce the cost of the public issue and enhance the business of the shares in the regional stock exchanges.

Table 5.10: Number of Listing

Types of MBs	*Agree*	*Undecided*	*Disagree*
AFI	1	–	–
SFI	–	–	1
NB	1	–	1
NBS	1	–	–
PSB	2	–	–
PMB	18	–	1
Total	23	–	3
%	(89)	–	(11)

(h) *Minimum Number of Shareholders*

The Bombay Stock Exchange has amended its listing requirements in accordance with SEBI guidelines. The amendment reads that a company has to have at least 5 public shareholders for every Rs. 1 lakh of net capital offer made to the public. The basic idea behind this measure of the Bombay Stock Exchange is to give more participation of the public shareholder in the company. But practically it is very difficult to observe the above guidelines by the issuer as well as the merchant-banker. Under the depressed primary market condition, the merchant-banker would find it difficult to get the required number of the application forms from the public shareholder. Further, the proportionate allotment system of SEBI is in contrast to this particular measure of the Bombay Stock Exchange. "SEBI's proportionate allotment requires a minimum of 50 per cent of the net offer of securities to the public to be made available for allotment to individual applicants who have applied for 1000 or less than 1000 securities and the balance of the net offer of securities to the public to be made available to investors, including corporate bodies' institutions and individual applicants who have applied for more than 1000 securities."[7] The researcher made a personal discussion with the private merchant-bankers, during the discussion they conferred that they fulfil this particular norm by way of just entering the names of the investors in the application form without receiving any money. This is done by splitting the original investors money into different names. Table 5.11 explains the views of the sampled merchant-bankers.

Table 5.11: Minimum Number of Shareholders

Types of MBs	*Very Useful*	*Of Average Use*	*Not Useful*
AFI	–	–	1
SFI	–	1	–
NB	2	–	–
NBS	–	–	1
PSB	1	–	1
PMB	6	5	8
Total	9	6	11
(%)	(35)	(23)	(42)

From Table 5.11, it is crystal clear that 42 per cent of the respondents viewed that the measure of the stock exchange was not useful. Six (23%) out of 26 opined that it had average use and 9 (35%) opined that it was very useful.

(c) Minimum Issued Capital

The minimum issued capital of a company for eligibility to list, was as low as Rs. 5 lakhs till November 2,1982. Guidelines issued by the Securities and Exchange Board of India on September 29, 1995 restricted the listing of companies with a commercial production of less than two years and with a post-public issue of paid up capital up to Rs. 5 crore only on those stock exchanges which have facility of screen-based trading. But the Bombay Stock Exchange recently amended the listing norms and says that the company eligible to list in Bombay Stock Exchange (BSE) should have a post-issue capital of Rs. 10 crore. The BSE administrators have enhanced the minimum equity capital from Rs. 3 crore to Rs. 10 crore in a short span of one year. In the past, minimum equity capital on listing was only Rs. 50 lakh which was raised to Rs. 3 crore over a period of 10 years.

This particular guideline of the BSE will affect the corporate sector as well as the merchant banking community. To observe the BSE guidelines, as most of the issuers will be either forced to go to the screen-based exchanges or regional exchanges or reduce the project cost to Rs. 10 crore. Listing shares with the regional stock exchanges or the screen-based (OTCEI) exchanges is not preferred by the issuer. The researcher elicited information about the Bombay Stock Exchange stipulation on the listing, and is presented in Table 5.12.

Table 5.12: Minimum Issued Capital

Types of MBs	*Very Useful*	*Of Average Use*	*Not Useful*
AFI	1	–	–
SFI	–	1	–
NB	1	1	–
NBS	1	–	–
PSB	1	1	–
PMB	11	3	5
Total	15	6	5
(%)	(58)	(23)	(19)

The Table 5.12 clearly shows that 58 per cent of the respondents have opined that the stipulation of the BSE was welcomable one and another 23% of the respondents had the opinion that it had average use. However, the five (19%) out of 26 have differed from the opinion and they stated that it was not useful.

Assistance in Settlement of Dues

(a) Settlement of Intermediaries Claims

There is undue delay in settlement of the brokerage, underwriting commission and fees to the merchant-bankers by the issuer. To safeguard the interest of the intermediaries, SEBI has directed the issuer to deposit 1 per cent of the public issue money in the regional stock exchanges. After clearing the dues to the intermediaries, the issuer can get back the security deposit from the regional stock exchanges. But SEBI has received numerous complaints that issuer companies have not paid dues to the underwriters, brokers, merchant-bankers and registrar and their 1 per cent security deposit has been released by the stock exchanges concerned. Hence the SEBI has directed the stock exchanges that they will now have to issue a certificate to the issuer company to the effect that underwriting and brokerage commission have been paid. The certificate from the regional stock exchange is a pre-requisite for the issue of a no-objection certificate by SEBI to release the 1 per cent security deposit placed in the regional stock exchanges. Table 5.13 gives the opinion about the merchant-bankers in this regard.

Table 5.13: Delay in Settlement of Intermediaries Claims

Types of MBs	*Agree*	*Undecided*	*Disagree*
AFI	1	–	–
SFI	–	1	–
NB	1	1	–
NBS	1	–	–
PSB	2	–	–
PMB	9	8	2
Total	14	10	2
(%)	(54)	(38)	(8)

It can be inferred from table 5.13 that 54 per cent of the respondents have agreed that there was delay in settlement of claims by the issuer. Another 38% of respondents are undecided and 8% disagreed.

(*b*) *Settlement of Lead Merchant Banker Fees*

It is the duty of the issuer to pay the agreed fees and other expenses to the merchant-banker after discharging the issue management function. There is a general opinion about the issuers that they are not remitting the fees and other expenses to various intermediaries. The underwriter and broker are unable to get their commission from the issuer. It is also reported that some of the merchant-bankers are not getting their fees and other charges from the issuer. Therefore, the researcher wanted to know whether the study units could get the fees and other expenses from the issuer or not. Table 5.14 portrays the opinion of the sampled merchant-bankers under study.

Table 5.14: Settlement of Lead Merchant-banker Fees

Types of MBs	*As per Agreement*		*Not as per Agreement*		*Total*
	In Time	*Not in Time*	*In time*	*Not in Time*	
AFI	1	–	–	–	1
SFI	1	–	–	–	1
NB	1	1	–	–	2
NBS	1	–	–	–	1
PSB	2	–	–	–	2
PMB	4	5	3	7	19
Total	10	6	3	7	26
(%)	(38)	(23)	(12)	(27)	(100)

Twenty-three per cent of the respondents have agreed that the issuers did not settle the fees and claims of the merchant-bankers in due time. Nearly 27 per cent have confirmed that the issuers did not settle the due amount either in due time or as agreement. It may be concluded that the 23 per cent of the merchant-bankers did not get their fees in due time and another 12 per cent of them did get their fees in time but not as per the agreement made with the issuer earlier.

REFERENCES

1. Hema Rajasekar, "Capital Issues–A Stock of Trouble", *The Economic Times,* (Bangalore Edition), 28th Feb 1991, p. 9.
2. Manoj Mitta, "Share Registrars feeling the heat", *India Today,* 30th June, 1995, p. 110.
3. *Manual of SEBI Guidelines,* Nabhi Publications, New Delhi, Sep. 1994, p. 382.
4. *Ibid.*, p. 382.
5. Manoj Mitta, *op. cit.*, p. 110.
6. Niranjan Rajadhuaksha and Bhupesh Bhandari, "Finance Goes Country Wide", *Business World,* 12th-25th June, 1996, p. 25.
7. M.R. Mayya, "Listing Norms—A Critique", *The Ecconomic Times,* 7th Sep, 1996 p. 4.

6

Impact of SEBI Measures

The new issue management exercise is governed by the provisions of so many enactment. It is necessary that issuer, lead merchant-banker and other intermediaries connected with the issue management services should possess adequate knowledge about the various rules and regulations. The following are the most important enactments with regard to the new issue management.

(a) The Companies Act, of 1956.

(b) The Securities and Exchange Board of India (SEBI) Act, 1992.

(c) The Securities Contracts (Regulation) Act, 1956.

(d) The Foreign Exchange Regulation Act 1973 as amended by Foreign Exchange Regulation (Amendment) Act, 1993.

(e) The Income Tax Act, 1961.

(f) The Wealth Tax Act, 1975.

(g) The Industries (Development and Regulation) Act, 1951.

Of the above all enactments, the SEBI Act, 1992 is very much relevant as far as the lead merchant-banker is concerned. Securities and Exchange Board of India (SEBI) was set up on April 12, 1988. The Government conferred statutory powers to SEBI by way of passing separate legislation in the name of SEBI Act, 1992. The important areas covered by SEBI are:

(i) Registration of bankers and sub-brokers in stock exchanges.

(ii) Authorisation of merchant-bankers.

(iii) Control of mutual funds.

(v) Issue of insider trading regulations.

(v) Issue of portfolio management regulations.

(vi) Issue of guidelines for disclosure and investor protection.

SEBI has issued a series of guidelines, clarifications, rules and regulations to develop, stabilise, consolidate the Indian Capital Market since 1992. Among the rules and regulations with regard to the lead merchant-bankers the SEBI (Merchant-bankers) Rules and Regulations, 1992 and SEBI (Disclosure and Investor Protection) Guidelines, 1992 are relevant to this study. Therefore, an attempt has been made to analyse the impact of SEBI, ROC, Stock Exchanges etc. guidelines and classification to the merchant-bankers.

Registration of Merchant-bankers

The SEBI Merchant-bankers Rules, 1992, Rule 3 provides that no person shall carry on any activity as a merchant-banker unless he holds a registration certificate granted by the SEBI.

Therefore, SEBI has made the registration of Merchant-bankers compulsory. Only professionals with requisite qualification, experience and capital adequacy can enter into the job. These Merchant-bankers are classified into four categories. The first category Merchant-bankers must have a minimum Capital adequacy (paid-up Capital and reserves) of Rs. 1 Crore. They can act as issue manager, advisor, consultant, underwriter and portfolio manager. The second category of merchant-bankers must have a minimum capital adequacy of Rs. 50 lakh. They can undertake all activities except issue management. The third category of Merchant-bankers must have a minimum capital adequacy of Rs. 20 lakh. They can act as underwriter, advisor and consultant. There is no Capital adequacy for fourth category of Merchant-bankers and they can function as advisor or consultant only. Hence for acting as merchant-banker, a certificate of registration from SEBI is necessary. But before the enactment of the SEBI Merchant-banker Rules, the Ministry of Finance had a control over the entire merchant banking community.

On granting a certificate the applicant is liable to pay the fees depending upon the category for which the registration is granted. Table 6.1 exhibits the fees for registration and renewals.

Table 6.1 Fees for Registration and Renewals

Category	*Registration*		*Renewal Fees*	
	1–2 Years Rs.	*Thereafter Rs.*	*1–2 Years Rs.*	*Thereafter Rs.*
I	2,00,000	1,00,000	1,00,000	20,000
II	1,50,000	50,000	75,000	10,000
III	1,00,000	25,000	50,000	5,000
IV	5,000	1,000	5,000	2,000

The certificate of the registration or its renewal is valid for a period of three years from the date of issue to the applicant. Instalments and renewal fees must be paid on or before the expiry of 12 months of each year of registration. Where a merchant-banker fails to pay the annual fees, the SEBI may suspend the registration certificate. As per September 1997 guidelines of SEBI, it has prohibited merchant-bankers from doing any of the fund-based activities. Banks and financial institutions are, however, exempt from this. Further, it has abolished the multiple categories of merchant-bankers, and allowing category I players to act as merchant-bankers provided they a net worth of Rs. 5 crore. Therefore, the registration fees, renewal fees and capital adequacy amount mentioned above are applicable to Category I Merchant-bankers alone.

Level of Fees

The lead manager (category I merchant-bankers) shall pay registration fees and renewal fees to the SEBI every year to keep his registration in force. For registration a sum of Rs. 2.5 lakh is to be paid annually by the lead manager for the first two years and thereafter for the third year a sum of

Rs. 1 lakh is to be paid. For renewal a sum of Rs. 1 lakh is to be paid annually by the lead manager for the first two years and thereafter for the third year a sum of Rs. 20,000 is to be paid. The merchant-bankers are constrained to get good amount of new issue mandate otherwise it is very difficult for them to pay the registration and renewal fees.

In this regard, the researcher wanted to ascertain whether the registration and renewal fees are normal or otherwise. For this purpose the researcher elicited information and that is put in the form of a table (Table 6.2).

Table 6.2: SEBI Registration and Renewal Fees

Types of Merchant-bankers	*Agree*	*Undecided*	*Disagree*
AFI	–	1	–
SFI	1	–	–
NB	1	–	1
NBS	–	1	–
PSB	–	1	1
PMB	10	5	4
Total	12	8	6
(%)	(46)	(31)	(23)

Of 26 Merchant-bankers, 6 alone stated that the registration and renewal fees were not normal. Forty-six per cent of the respondents under study agreed that the registration and renewal fees were normal. At the time of personal discussion with the merchant-bankers, most of them opined that SEBI should give some grace time to remit the renewal fees. They also expressed that SEBI should intimate the expiry time or the renewal time to the merchant-bankers. This will reduce the default of remittance of the renewal fees.

Number of Lead Merchant-bankers to an Issue

Every issue should be managed by at least one merchant-banker. The appointment of a lead merchant-banker shall not be essential for rights issue which is below 50 lakh.

The maximum number of lead merchant-bankers allotted for an issue depends on the size of the issue. These are 2

Merchant-bankers for below Rs. 50 crore, 3 for below Rs. 100 crore, 4 for below Rs. 200 crore and 5 for below Rs. 400 crore.

Depending upon the size of the issue, the issuer can select a lead manager or more than one lead manager for the proposed public issue. Almost invariably the merchant-banker is appointed by the company not because of his skill in financial structuring, pricing and distribution, but because of other considerations namely bridge loan, project finance, etc. The merchant-banker may have had a better relationship with the issue with regard to services already availed, which may have influenced the choice. On certain occasions, financial institutions stipulate that they will manage the issue simply because they provide funds for the project. However, the prospective issuers are not entirely dependent on the financial institutions/banks based merchant-bankers and they are also appointing the small merchant-bankers together with the financial institutions/banks based merchant-bankers. It may be appropriate to quote "Since most of the issuers of large bonds are Public Sector Undertakings, they appoint at least one merchant banking outfit of a leading financial institution/ bank. They also select private sector merchant banks in view of their distribution strengths".[1]

Further, if the issuer feels the need for appointing additional lead merchant-bankers for post-issue activities as a reciprocal for the favours done in the past, then a lead merchant-banker is supported by co-lead merchant-banker even though the size is not warranted. Therefore, the merchant-banker focuses his strength either on project finance of distribution capability or relationship banking which will lead to either lead managing mandate for pre-issue activities or post-issue activities.

Impact of Multiple and Single Lead Merchant-bankers

Based on size of the issue SEBI has allowed more than one lead merchant-bankers to participate in an issue. Therefore there is a general perception that if more number of lead merchant-bankers participate in an issue, the issue is a good one. To verify whether there was a significant difference between the issues handled by the lead merchant-bankers collectively and solely, the researcher classified the issues handled by the sample lead merchant-bankers during 1.1.96 to 30.6.96 into two different groups namely multiple merchant-bankers and single merchant-bankers. The correlation coefficient between Issue Price (IP) and Market Price (MP) of the above two groups and the t-test results of the same are given in Table 6.3.

Table 6.3 Correlation Coefficient Results

Types of MBs	*Values*			*d.f at*	*Results*
	r	*t*	*critical*	*0.01 level*	
Multiple Merchant bankers	0.48	2.176	2.921	16	Positive Relationship and No Significance
Single Merchant Bankers	0.34	1.1826	4.032	05	Positive Relationship and No Significance

The correlation coefficient of IP and MP in both the cases were positive. For the issue of those merchant-bankers who handled the issues collectively, the correlation coefficient was high (0.48), when compared to merchant-bankers who handled the issues solely. It is inferred that the association between IP and MP had no significance in the case of issues handled by the multiple lead merchant-bankers. It may be concluded that there was a lesser possibility of thorough due diligence on the part of the multiple merchant-bankers. This sets the stage for rigorous evaluation of the performance of the lead merchant-bankers who have handled the issues solely in different angles. That is the association between the performance of the lead merchant-

Table 6.4: t-test results for Hypothesis

Relationship between	*Values*		*d.f at*	*Results*
	t	*critical*	*0.01 level*	
Multiple and Single Merchant bankers	0.254	2.807	23	No Significance

bankers who have handled issues solely and multiply was tested using the student t-test. The results of the above analysis are presented in Table 6.4.

Since the difference between the 2 sample means lies inside the acceptance limit therefore, the null hypothesis is accepted. Hence it is concluded that the performance of the lead merchant-bankers who had handled the issues multiply did not differ significantly from those who had handled issues solely.

Reduction of Number and Category of Merchant Bankers

One of the major criticism directed against merchant banking industry is the plethora of players operating in the merchant banking industry. There are around 1,163 merchant-bankers with varying stature and size operating in the industry. In many developed and developing markets, the number is small. The principle of survival of the fittest will come into play. Merchant banking requires skill and relationships. Mere set up of office does not necessarily ensure business. Ambi Chairman and IDBI executive director Mr. Taparia has rightly pointed out "Only about two dozen merchant-bankers do most of the business."[2] Therefore, the question in our mind is that is it necessary to have large number of merchant-bankers in the industry. In this regard the views of the merchant-bankers were obtained. Their views are presented in Table 6.5.

Table 6.5: Reduction of Number and Category of Merchant-bankers

Merchant-banker Group	*Agree*	*Undecided*	*Disagree*
SFI	1	–	–
SFI	1	–	–
NB	2	–	–
NBS	1	–	–
PSB	2	–	–
PMB	12	3	4
Total (%)	19 (73)	3 (12)	4 (15)

It is interesting to state that majority (73%) of the merchant-bankers agreed that there should be some reduction in the number of merchant-bankers in the industry. They also welcomed the recent measure on abolition of the category II, III, and IV merchant-bankers by SEBI.

Procedure for Inspection

SEBI may inspect books of accounts, records and documents of merchant-bankers to ensure their maintenance in the required manner. SEBI may appoint a qualified Auditor to investigate into the books of account or affairs of the merchant-banker. Penalties for non-compliance of conditions for registration and contravention of the provisions of the merchant-bankers regulation include suspension or cancellation of registration. For this purpose, a system of imposing penalty points was introduced by SEBI to the Merchant-bankers who violate the terms of their authorisation. The detailed penalty provision are contained in SEBI (Merchant-bankers) Regulations, 1992.

In this regulation, the generally observed areas of non-compliance/defaults have been categorised into four areas namely general defaults, minor defaults, major defaults and serious defaults. The penalty points for the above mentioned four defaults are namely 1, 2, 3 and 4 respectively.

Before awarding penalty point(s), SEBI will inform the concerned merchant-banker for representation. Maximum penalty points awarded in a single issue managed by a merchant-banker shall be restricted to four. The penalty point shall be awarded to the lead manager responsible for the concerned activities. In the event of the joint responsibilities, same penalty point shall be awarded to all lead mangers jointly responsible for the activity.

A merchant-banker on reaching cumulative penalty points of eight shall attract action from SEBI. However, SEBI has reserved the right to take immediate action against any merchant-banker, without award of any penalty points but it warrants immediate action.

Inspection of Merchant-bankers

SEBI has launched an inspection of 30 top merchant-bankers for the first time in September 1996, to evaluate their due diligence capability after giving up its vetting powers to merchant-bankers. The inspection reports showed how the promoters and the merchant-bankers colluded to push the public issues. Further with the help of the Financial Institutions Reform and Expansion (FIRE) project of Price Water house, SEBI has worked out a list of details seeking from all Category I of merchant-bankers. "Earlier we were monitoring the merchant-bankers on an entity level, now we will be monitoring them on an employee level",[3] says SEBI source. If vetting of offer document by SEBI is abolished, it follows that the merchant-bankers must accept greater responsibility for the issues they bring to the market. These measures appear to be a right move towards the greater regulation in the Primary market. But how the merchant-bankers reacted to this move is ascertained through the questionnaire. The information about the merchant-bankers are presented in Table 6.6.

Table 6.6: Inspection of Merchant-bankers

Merchant Group	*Agree*	*Undecided*	*Disagree*
AFI	1	–	–
SFI	1	–	–
NB	2	–	–
NBS	1	–	–
PSB	2	–	–
PMB	16	2	1
Total	23	2	1
(%)	(88)	(8)	(4)

It is very interesting to note from the Table 6.6 that 23 (88%) out of 26 merchant-bankers accepted the inspection move of the SEBI. Only one merchant-banker disagreed with this particular move. It is concluded that the merchant banking community was willing to accept the responsibility and wanted to make their deal in a transparent manner.

Entry Norm to Issuer

According to SEBI, an issuer company must have a track record of dividend payment for at least three years for going public. Under this regulation, the term 'track record' has not been defined and has therefore been misused. Certain companies have been found to have declared dividend with retrospective effect and then brought out a public issue. Therefore, SEBI has been forced to plug a few loopholes in the regulation. A company which plans to tap the primary market should have declared dividends in the relevant three consecutive previous years. 'Track Record' would now mean that the record has been created in the relevant years themselves. It is everybody's interest to know whether this particular stipulation is quite useful or not. In this regard the researcher gathered valid information from the sampled merchant banking community. It is presented in Table 6.7.

Table 6.7: Entry Norm to Issuer

Types of Merchant-bankers	*Very Useful*	*Of Average Use*	*Not Useful*
AFI	–	1	–
SFI	1	–	–
NB	2	–	–
NBS	–	1	–
PSB	1	1	–
PMB	13	3	3
Total	17	6	3
(%)	(65)	(23)	(12)

It is inferred from the Table 6.7 that 88 per cent of the respondents agreed that the entry norm was very useful to issuer.

Significance of Entry Norm

The new companies can issue shares to the public only at par. However the new companies can issue shares to the public at a premium if the new companies have a 5 year track record of consistent profitability. In the case of existing private company or unlisted company which issue shares to the public for the first time it should have track record of consistent profitability for three years. The above stipulation was practised until April 1996. Many companies have misused the above criteria and large number of "dud" issues hit the market.

Therefore, on April 17, 1996, SEBI has stipulated, based on the recommendation of Y.H. Malegam Committee, that the company must have a track record of dividend payment for at least three years for going public. This norm restricted the issuers from going to public considerably. Here it is worthwhile to mention the study conducted by the Prime Database. The study states that "of the 1428 public issues that tapped the capital market in 1995-96, only 399 would have qualified under the new guidelines. There is a drop of 72 per cent-and it's an indication of the poor quality of the issues that hit the market."[4] There is a belief that this SEBI's norm may improve the quality of the issue, to verify the above belief and know the association between the issues before SEBI's norms and after SEBI's norm, an analysis has been carried out. For this purpose, the researcher classified the issues handled by the sampled lead merchant-bankers during 1.1.96 to 30.6.96 into two different groups namely issues before the SEBI's entry norm and issues after the SEBI's entry norm.

The correlation coefficient between Issue Price (IP) and Market Price (MP) of above two periods and the t-test of the above two and the results of the same are given in Table 6.8.

Table 6.8: Correlation Coefficient Results

Groups	*Values*			*d.f at*	*Results*
	r	*t*	*critical*	*0.01 level*	
Before SEBI's Norms	0.33	1.209	3.055	12	Positive relationship and No Significance
After SEBI's Norms	0.52	1.8266	3.250	09	Positive relationship and No Significance

The correlation of IP and MP in both the cases were positive but for those companies which made public offering after the SEBI's norm, the correlation was high (0.52), when compared to public issues before the SEBI' norm. It is very clear that the association between IP and MP was not significant. It is construed that there was some impact of the SEBI's new guidelines. This sets the stage for rigorous evaluation of lead merchant-bankers performance in different angles. That is the association between the sample merchant-bankers who have handled issues after the SEBI norms and before the SEBI norms. For this purpose the student t-test is applied to test the difference between the mean values. The results of the above analysis is presented in Table 6.9.

Table 6.9: t-test result for Hypothesis

Relationship between	*Values*		*d.f at 0.01 level*	*Results*
	t	*critical*		
Before SEBI's norms and after SEBI's norms	0.345	2.807	23	No Significance

Since the difference between the 2 sample means lies inside the acceptance region, the null hypothesis is accepted and hence it is concluded that the performance of the merchant-bankers who have handled the issues after the SEBI's entry norm i.e. three year track record of dividend payment did not differ significantly from those who have handled issues before to such norm of SEBI.

Promoters' Contribution and Lock-in-Period

Promoters shall bring in their contribution in full in advance before the opening up of the issue. Promoters' contribution can be brought in by persons described as promoters in the prospectus, directors of the company, friends and relatives of the directors and business associates. The minimum amount that these persons have to bring to qualify for promoters contribution is Rs. 25,000 each. However, in the case of business associates the minimum amount is Rs. 1,00,000. The earlier guideline of the SEBI states that the promoters' contribution has been subjected to a lock in period of 5 years from the date of allotment or if the company is manufacturing company, from the date of allotment or date of commercial production.

The SEBI's guidelines on 14th May 1997, modified the provision of lock-in-period of the promoters. In the case of rights issues at a premium, the requirement of promoters' contribution and lock-in-period will no longer be applicable. In cases of preferential issues (as per SEBI guidelines dated 4th August, 1994) and public issues, wherever the provision of lock-in period of promoters' contribution are applicable for a period of 5 years, the same shall be reduced uniformly for a period of 3 years. No doubt, this particular modification is largely useful to issuer. At the same time existing companies' promoters are coming forward to make the fresh issue and in turn it will give business to the merchant-banker. Further, the existing company promoters can sell the excess share-holding in the company and get funds from the secondary market and can start the new venture.

As per the new guidelines of the SEBI, the promoters' contribution of 25 per cent is not required for the promoter of a listed company having a track record of three years of profitable operations. It shall not be less than 20 per cent of the issue. From the promoters' angle, this is a good move, as the promoter need not keep his money locked in when the same could be better utilised elsewhere. The impact of the SEBI's decision on reduction in lock-in-period and minimum contribution for promoter's stake on the new issue management was ascertained, and it is presented in Table 6.10.

Table 6.10: Promoter's Stake and Lock in Period

Types of Merchant-bankers	*Very Useful*	*Of Average Use*	*Not Useful*
AFI	1	–	–
SFI	–	1	–
NB	1	1	–
NBS	–	1	–
PSB	2	–	–
PMB	10	2	7
Total	14	5	7
(%)	(54)	(19)	(27)

Only 54 per cent of the respondents had the feeling that this reduction of the lock-in-period as well as the contribution was very useful to promote the new issue business. The remaining 46 per cent held the view that these measures would not induce the promoter to make the new issue. This might be due to the depressed condition of the secondary market. The secondary market is not very active. The promoters may not be able to sell their holdings at a higher price and ultimately they may not come forward to make any fresh issue. During the personal interviews with the private merchant-bankers, it was observed that most of the promoters are willing to hold larger share in the company in order to avoid the hostile takeover bids by the predators.

Cost of Public Issue

Before giving the mandate to merchant-banker the issuer seeks the proposed budget for the issue cost. Based on the budget the issuer can estimate the cost of raising the funds. The cost of raising the funds should be minimum so that issuer can effectively utilise the funds in the project. The public issue cost can be split up into two namely mandatory cost and non-mandatory cost. Mandatory costs are those costs which are incurred for brokerage, underwriting commission, listing fees, issue manager fees, registrar fees and mandatory advertisement charges on the distribution of various financial instruments to the target market in order to raise funds. The non-mandatory costs generally include the following: Printing of prospectus, brochures, application forms, pads, publicity, issue advertisement, conference and hoardings etc. Hence, information about the estimated average, mandatory and non-mandatory public issue cost Rs. 5 crore of an issue was elicited from the merchant-bankers under study. The respondents views on these are given in Table 6.11.

From Table 6.11 it is inferred that out of 26 merchant-bankers under study, 19 private merchant-bankers opined that the total estimated cost of public issue might be around 15 per cent. Further, the nationalised banks and state financial institutions opined that the cost might be around 11 to 12 per cent. But the All India Financial Institution, private sector bank, and nationalised bank subsidiary have quoted that the estimated cost might be around 9 per cent. This might be due to factors like the branch network facilities, infra-structural facilities and aids from the parent organisation to these institutions.

Table 6.11: The Estimated Public Issue Cost (% to issue size)

Types of Merchant Bankers	*Average Mandatory Cost (%)*	*Average Non-Mandatory Cost (%)*	*Total*
AFI (1)	6	3	9
SFI (1)	7	5	12
NB (2)	6	5	11
NBS (1)	6	3	9
PSB (2)	6	3	9
PMB (19)	10	5	15

Note: Figures in parenthesis refer to number of merchant-bankers

Difference in Public Issue Cost

The Public issue cost is disclosed in the offer documents. The cost mentioned in the offer document is a tentative one. The actual public issue expenditure may be more than the cost mentioned in the offer document. The general practice of issuing company is to mention the statutory percentage of public issue cost in the books of accounts. The excess cost includes the transportation, travel, general administrative expenses, and general advertising expenditure. The Table show 6.12 the cost of public issue mentioned in the offer documents of the issues handled by sample merchant-bankers' of 148 Companies.

Table 6.12: Cost of Public Issue in offer Document

Issue Cost in Percentage	*Types of Merchant-bankers*						*No. of Companies*
	AFI	*SFI*	*NB*	*NBS*	*PSB*	*PMB*	
Below 6	1	–	1	3	–	18	23
6-9	2	1	1	3	–	47	54
9-12	–	–	1	1	–	22	24
12-15	–	–	–	–	–	5	5
15-18	–	–	–	–	–	30	30
Above 18	–	–	–	–	–	12	12
Total	3	1	3	7	–	134	148

Source: Complied from Prospectus of the Companies which made Public Issue between January 1996 and June 1996.

Majority of the (69%) of the companies mentioned public issue cost below 9 per cent. But the average public issue cost of the existing and new companies was ranging between 15 and 20 during the period 1986–1996 (see Annexure XIV). The sampled merchant-bankers opined that there were differences in actual and estimated cost and they suggested the issuer to adjust the excess expenditure in the administrative and travel expenses. Therefore, it is evident that the actual public issue cost is more than the cost mentioned in the offer document. Hence, it is essential to revise the policy applicable to non-mandatory cost percentage.

Revision of Public Issue Cost

As per the guidelines of the SEBI, the issuer and merchant-banker are much worried about the ever increasing public issue cost. They are in a position to observe the following important guidelines pertaining to the issue process. (1) An abridged prospectus needs to be attached to every share application form. (2) Share certificate and refund orders have to be sent by registered post. (3) Interest (15%) has to be paid by companies to the investors on delayed refunds. These guidelines have major cost implications, the most important being the requirement of the abridged prospectus be attached to the application form. It was provided by the Securities Contracts (Regulation) Act, 1956, at the time of enactment of the Act, and SEBI has revived it in 1991. The number of shareholders then was small and manageable, and any company issuing shares typically did not have to print more than a few thousand application forms. But as the number of shareholders rose, it is required to print more than a lakh application forms. Merchant-bankers estimate that printing a single application form-cum-prospectus will cost 50 paise. Suppose printing of one crore forms would thus cost Rs. 50 lakh. Further, merchant-bankers estimate that refund orders and share certificates should be sent by registered post which adds Rs. 11 per envelope, resulting in an extra Rs. 55 lakhs if there are five lakh mailings.

Generally, the investors' response rate is a mere two to four per cent of the number of share application forms printed and distributed. Although, this may not be a big problem to the blue-chip companies with good projects. It will be certainly disastrous for the companies which are entering into the capital market for the first time.

The overall ceiling on the amount of expenditure on public issues of capital should be the following: (1) For the Equity and Convertible debenture upto Rs. 5 crore, it is Mandatory cost plus 5 per cent. For more than Rs. 5 crore it is Mandatory cost plus 2 per cent. (2) For non-convertible debentures upto Rs. 5 crore, it is Mandatory cost plug 2 per cent and in excess of Rs. 5 crore, it will be Mandatory cost plus 1 per cent. Table 6.13 shows the opinion of the sample units with regard to the revisions of overall ceiling of public issue cost.

Table 6.13: Revision of Public Issue Cost

Types of Merchant-bankers	*Agree*	*Undecided*	*Disagree*
AFI	1	–	–
SFI	–	1	–
NB	–	1	1
NBS	1	–	–
PSB	1	–	1
PMB	18	1	–
Total	21	3	2
(%)	(81)	(11)	(8)

It is inferred from Table 6.13 that 81 per cent of the respondents held the view that the existing public issue cost percentage in respect on non-mandatory cost was not adequate. Ever increasing stationary and printing charges, distribution, postage and advertisement charges make essential need to revise the overall limit on the non-mandatory public issue cost.

Mandatory Underwriting

Initially, the SEBI made, underwriting as mandatory for all the Public Issues. Then from October 1994 onwards, underwriting is not mandatory. This has reduced the underwriting business and also has caused difficulties to the new issue. For example, "47 of the 150 issues that entered the Primary Market in January 1995-or 63% of the amount raised-were not underwritten. By contrast, just 1.8 per cent of new issues-14% of the amount raised went-underwritten in 1993-94".[5] This freedom causes a lot of problems for the lead-managers and it leads to postponement of issue closing dates. Further, in 1995-96, according to the Primary Market Monitor, "334 of the 1428 public issues (including debt) that opened for subscription could not close on the earliest closing date. Only 30 per cent of the total issued amount of Rs. 10980 crore was underwritten, as against 77 per cent in 1994-95. The first half of the current year (1995-96) kept up the sad pace. There's no underwriting business today", admits SBI Capital Markets Limited managing director A. R. Barwe.[6] The above facts really cause concern to the merchant-bankers because the primary market is already at a comatose, and the public investors do not turn their faces to the new issue market. If the underwriting is not mandatory, there is no scope for the new entrepreneurs to add vigour and strength in their project. The researcher inquired in this regard to the sampled merchant-bankers under study. Their views are expressed in Table 6.14 below.

Table 6.14: Needs of Mandatory Underwriting

Types of Merchant-bankers	*Agree*	*Undecided*	*Disagree*
AFI	1	–	–
SFI	1	–	–
NB	1	1	–
NBS	–	–	1
PSB	–	1	1
PMB	8	5	6
Total	11	7	8
(%)	(42)	(27)	(31)

From Table 6.14, one can infer that 11 out of 26 (42 per cent) of the respondents felt that the mandatory underwriting was needed for the success of the issue. But seven out of 26 were indifferent. Another 8 out of 26 were in the category of disagree. The private merchant-bankers and Nationalised Bank subsidiary and private sector bank were under the disagree category. The reason for disagreement was asked by the researcher during the personal interview and they opined that as far as India was concerned the underwriters operated as investors than as underwriters.

Commitment in Underwriting

Subscription or Oversubscription are the twin terms worshipped by promoters, merchant-bankers and to some extent, even by the investing public. Since (October 1994) the mandatory underwriting removed by the SEBI, "81 per cent of the issues in 1994-95 was underwritten. In 1995-96 the figure fell to 31%".[7] At present the primary market condition is dismal and the underwriting business is nil in most of the cases. But it is very surprising to the general public that there is no much public advertisement about the development except only in the large issues like Chambal Fertilisers, Usha Rectifiers, Bhushan Steel and Strips, Malvika, Cipla, Pittee etc., during the period 1995-1996.

The development of the issues like Chambal Fertilizer, Malvika, Bhushan Steel and Strips etc., has scared the underwriters, who have now started rejecting underwriting offers on a large scale. The top brokers have decided to withdraw underwriting commitments in 80 issues. The issues where underwriting has been withdrawn comprise the ones not filed before Registrar of Companies. Merchant-banker said, "No underwriter is willing to pay up and various alibis are found to dodge commitments".[8] Apart from shouldering the responsibility of issue management, the lead manager is also bearing the responsibility to accept a minimum underwriting obligation of 5 per cent of the total underwriting commitment or Rs. 25 lakh whichever is less. The SEBI has allowed the Category I, II and III merchant-bankers to act as underwriters. Further, it is noted that SEBI has issued notices to 134 merchant-bankers for cancellation and suspension of merchant banking licenses for not honouring their underwriting commitments in public issues.

Out of 134 merchant-bankers 9 are Commercial Banks. "Underwriting had ceased to have any meaning as intermediaries were not bothered about fulfilling the devolvements and only earned commissions if the issue was subscribed, sources said."[9] Hence the underwriters, brokers, merchant-bankers have not accepted the commitments and if possible they are escaping from the commitments. Therefore, it is worthwhile to collect the opinion from the merchant-banker under study about the commitment in underwriting contract. The information gathered from the sampled units are presented in Table 6.15.

Table 6.15: Commitment in Underwriting

Types of Merchant-bankers	*Very Useful*	*Of Average Use*	*Not Useful*
AFI	1	–	–
SFI	1	–	–
NB	1	1	–
NBS	1	–	–
PSB	2	–	–
PMB	18	1	–
Total	24	2	–
(%)	(92)	(8)	–

Ninety-two per cent of the respondents have strongly agreed that the broker community and underwriters were not ready to accept the devolvement. It gave a great difficulty to the merchant-bankers to find the honest underwriters and brokers to make the issue success.

Mandatory Collection Centres

The Collecting branches send application forms and the forms received by them to a specified branch, where such details of the applications are consolidate. Such a specified branch of the Bankers to the issue is called "Controlling Branch". The progress of the daily collections and the receipt of the share applications are reported by these collecting branches to the controlling branch of the bank and also to the registrar to the issue.

The lead merchant-banker monitor the daily totals of applications received. The subscription list should be kept open for a minimum period of 3 working days. Depending upon the subscription level, the issuer will decide to close the subscription on the earliest date of closure or extend the date on the advice of the lead manager/registrar to the issue.

Formerly, the company had to make allotments to the public within 70 days of the closure of the public issue. But now, the Stock Exchanges have permitted company to make allotments to the public within 30 days. Generally, the issuer merchant-bankers and registrars have blamed the banker to the issue for the delay in the allotment of shares to the public. Now, the number of days has been reduced, it is very difficult to the registrar to get the relevant collection particulars from the bankers to the issue. Hence, the researcher obtained opinion regarding the reduction of the mandatory collection by the SEBI. The opinion of the sampled merchant-bankers are demonstrated in Table 6.16.

Table 6.16: Mandatory Collection Centre

Types of Merchant-bankers	*Agree*	*Undecided*	*Disagree*
AFI	1	–	–
SFI	–	–	1
NB	–	1	1
NBS	1	–	–
PSB	1	–	1
PMB	3	6	10
Total	6	7	13
(%)	(23)	(27)	(50)

Nearly 50 per cent of the respondents had the opinion that there was no need for further reduction of the collection centres. Six (i.e. 23%) out of 26 only had the opinion that the revision was needed. The reason may be due to the introduction of the collection agents in the new issue process. The merchant-banker in consultation with the issuer can appoint anybody who has banking service exposure as collection agents and they report the collection details quickly.

Management of Shortfall

Securities and Exchange Board of India has decided to extend the facility of procuring subscription within 60 days of the closure of an issue to promoters coming out with non-underwritten public issues. It means the promoters can now bring-in their own money or procure subscription from their association or other sources within 60 days of the closure of the issue. This move is widely accepted as a positive step towards boosting primary markets by the merchant-bankers as well as the issuers. The impact of this decision of the SEBI was checked by presenting a questionnaire to the respondents. The view of the respondents are presented in Table 6.17

Table 6.17: Management of Short Fall

Types of Merchant-bankers	*Very Useful*	*Of Average Use*	*Not Useful*
AFI	1	–	–
SFI	1	–	–
NB	2	–	–
NBS	–	1	–
FSB	2	–	–
PMB	17	2	–
Total	23	3	–
(%)	(88)	(12)	–

From Table 6.17 it is concluded that this particular step was absolutely essential for the development of the market. Twenty-three (88%) out of 26 respondents felt that the decision of the SEBI was very useful.

Approval from Stock Exchanges

The basis of allotment suggested by the lead management to the issue is placed before the Regional Stock Exchange for approval. The stock exchange scrutinises the proposed basis of allotment and suggests modifications, if any, on the basis which should be carried out. The researcher wanted to know whether there was any delay on the part of stock exchange in giving approval of the allotment. Table 6.18 below highlights the opinion of the merchant-bankers in this regard.

It can be inferred from Table 6.18 that only 5 (19%) merchant-bankers confirmed that there was some delay in the stock exchanges to approve the allotment. Rest of the merchant-

Table 6.18: Approval from SEs

Types of Merchant Bankers	*Agree*	*Undecided*	*Disagree*
AFI	–	–	1
SFI	–	1	–
NB	–	1	1
NBS	–	1	–
PSB	–	1	1
PMB	5	6	8
Total	5	10	11
(%)	(19)	(38)	(43)

bankers were under the undecided group (38%) and disagree (43%) group.

Factors Influencing Success of the Issue

Even though the merchant-bankers are precisely conducting the issue management activities, the success of the issue does not rest in their hands. Because the success or failure of the issue depends on so many factors. According to R.S. Bhatt "The new issue market receives a number of issues which are floated during the year. The success of each issue could depend first on the merits of the proposal, the prestige and reputation of the company, sponsorship of the issue house, and underwriters and finally on the investment climate at the time of the issue. Even though good issue may fail in adverse circumstances".[10] It is necessary to understand the basic factors which influence the success of issue management. The researcher has identified some of the factor which are having major influence on the success of the issue and included those factors in the questionnaire and gathered respondents preference on those factors and the overall weighted average score was found out. It is represented in Table 6.19.

As per Table 6.19, the respondents have disclosed that among other factors, the two primary factors which had stronger influence on the success of the issues were brokers network and company track record. These two factors' overall

Table 6.19: Factors Influencing the Success of the Issue

Factors	*Types of Merchant Banker (Weighted Average Score)*						*Overall Weighted*
	AFI	*SFI*	*NB*	*NBS*	*PSB*	*PMB*	*Avg. Score*
Broker Net Work	8	7	6.0	8.0	7.5	5.95	6.27
Investor's Preference	3	3	7.0	3.0	3.5	5.79	5.38
Advertising Influence	2	2	3.5	2.0	3.5	4.05	3.73
Company Track Record	4	8	7.0	7.0	6.5	5.89	6.07
Secondary Market Trend	6	6	3.5	6.0	4.5	4.95	4.92
Underwriter Arrangement	5	4	2.5	4.0	4.5	3.32	3.50
Issuers Strength	7	5	5.5	5.0	5.0	3.37	3.92
Issue Financier	1	1	1.0	1.0	1.0	2.63	2.19

weighted average score were 6.27 and 6.07 respectively. These two factors had some relationship. For example, if the brokers try to convince investors, they have to show the results of the issuer, then only the investors are inclined to invest their money in share of company, and the issue may prove to be a success. For convincing the investors, the brokers should give valid reason. That reason is the company track record of profitability, dividend payment and leadership in the business etc. It might be concluded that the brokers and company track record were the two influential factors which decide the success of the issue. The third important factor which was responsible for the success of the issue is the investor's preference. It also had equal footing in the success of the issue because the investor's preference was the basic aspect. If investors preference was positive, the issue be it good or bad will automatically become a success.

Frequent Changes in SEBI's Norms

SEBI plays an active role once it has acquired statutory powers. In record time it issued a plethora of guidelines and regulations. SEBI attempted to take on several issues but most of them were incomplete as clarifications were constantly added to the guidelines, which were often confusing. To quote, "If anything, SEBI could only be accused of forging ahead with great speed, with or without government backing, often defeating its own purpose. For example, guidelines for investor protection dated 11 June 1992, had to be followed up with more than six clarifications then, learning to a lot of confusion".[11] As Vijay Mehta, Chairman of Mefcom Capital Markets Limited has rightly pointed out that," "As a merchant-banker with 12 years' track record. I submit that frequent changes and tinkering with policies and with the issue of clarification after clarification creates confusion with most players not having a clear idea about the policy. Unless a long term policy is evolved, most of the difficulties faced by the players in the primary market will continue."[12] This evinced interest to the researcher to seek information about the frequent changes in SEBI's regulation from the study units. Their opinion is represented in Table 6.20.

Table 6.20: Frequent Changes in SEBI's Norms

Types of Merchant-bankers	*Agree*	*Undecided*	*Disagree*
AFI	–	–	1
SFI	1	–	–
NB	1	1	–
NBS	–	–	1
PSB	–	–	2
PMB	7	8	4
Total	9	9	8
(%)	(35)	(35)	(30)

It clearly shows that only 9 (35%) respondents agreed that too many clarifications of the SEBI spoiled the primary market growth. Nine (35%) out of 26 respondents were undecided about the frequent changes in SEBI's norms that spoiled the primary market.

Reasons for Sluggish Primary Market

At present the primary market is inactive. A lot of investors have burnt their fingers in the primary market. "A conservative estimate puts the paper losses of investors in premium issues over the past year (1994-95) at well over Rs. 12,000 crores".[13] Now the question is, Who is responsible for the sluggish primary market? May be the investors' over-confidence and greed or the promoters making the dud issues in the past or the merchant-bankers' failure to observe due diligence or the Government's failure to control the issuer and intermediaries. Actually, each one is responsible in varying degrees for the sluggish primary market at present. The researcher tried to elicit the reasons for the sluggish primary market prevailing at present. The merchant-bankers expressed their opinion and it is presented in Table 6.21.

Table 6.21: Reasons for Sluggish Primary Market

Reasons	*Types of Merchant-banker (Weighted Average Score)*						*Overall Weighted*
	AFI	*SFI*	*NB*	*NBS*	*PSB*	*PMB*	*Avg. Score*
Free Pricing	1	7	6.5	1.0	5.0	9.58	6.76
Ill–Liquidity	2	10	7.0	2.0	7.0	8.58	7.88
Due issues	7	11	8.0	11.0	8.5	8.05	8.26
Free Entry Norms	6	1	4.5	6.0	7.5	6.63	6.26
Projection Failed	11	5	8.0	10.0	8.5	6.32	6.88
Eco. and Political	4	9	8.0	3.0	6.5	7.37	7.99
Shift from Equity	5	3	5.5	5.0	5.5	5.68	5.50
Investor's Average	3	6	8.0	4.0	1.5	4.95	4.85
SEBI's Stringency	8	4	2.0	9.0	5.5	4.47	4.65
Free entry of MBs	9	2	3.0	8.0	6.0	2.74	3.42
Promoter's Greed	10	8	5.5	7.0	4.5	3.84	4.38

However, based on the information in Table 6.21 it is inferred that there had been six basic reasons for sluggishness in the primary market. They were: (1) Dud issues in the past (2) Ill-liquidity (3) Economic and Political reasons (4) Projections failed (5) Free Pricing and (6) Free Entry norms to the issuer and the respective overall weighted average score were 8.26, 7.88, 7.99, 6.88, 6.76 and 6.26. Among the six reasons the highest overall weighted average score secured (8.26) by dud issues in the past. In this case, the entire blame did not go to the issuer as the merchant-bankers were also party responsible for it as the merchant-bankers prepare the ground work and allow the issue to be floated in the market.

REFERENCES

1. Ken source information services private limited, "Marketing the Mega Issues", *The Merchant-bankers Update, Jan. 1997*, p. 27.
2. Ashok Jainani, "Merchant-bankers' tribe may be on the verge of extinction", *The Economic Times,* 16th September, 1997, p. 12.
3. Aruna Vaidyanathan, "SEBI turns the heat on merchant-bankers". *Business World,* May 1996, p. 32.
4. Rajiv Vyas, "Guillotined by the New guidelines", *Business World,* 15th-28th May 1996, p. 110.
5. Sunit Arora, "The Top Underwriters", *Business Today,* 22nd April 6th May, 1995 p. 128.
6. Vivek Bhargava, *op. cit.* p. 1.
7. Sandy Dias et al., "Small is Out", *Business World,* 4th-17th September, 1996. p. 36
8. Sanjeev Sharma, "Brokers Backout of Underwriting Commitments in 80 Issues", *The Economic Times,* 5th May, 1995, p. 1.
9. Sanjeev Sharma, "SEBI Notice to 9 Banks Among 134 Merchant-bankers", *The Economic Times,* 19th June, 1997, p. 3.
10. R.S. Bhatt, "The Indian Capital Market", *Economic and Social Development,* (Ed) S.L.N. Simha, Vora and Company Publisher, Delhi, p. 216.
11. Lancelot Joseph, "So much Stronger", *Business India,* 9th-22nd March, 1998, p. 202.
12. J.N. Kapur, *op. cit.,* p. 18.
13. Govindaraj Ethiraj and Bhupesh Bandari, "The Great Primary Market Rip-offs", *Business World,* 28th June-11th July, 1995, p. 36.

7

Merchant Bankers—Performance Analysis

An analysis on the role of the lead merchant-bankers in the new issue management can be studied in two ways. The first way is to study the statistics of the annual volume of new issues. These data may be broken into different types-for example, type of securities issued, method of flotation, type of instruments and so on. The Reserve Bank of India has been conducting a study on this line. However, this is a partial way and it does not disclose the level of efficiency of the lead merchant-bankers. In another way one can study the level of efficiency of merchant-bankers. In this second way, the issue price of the issues handled by the lead merchant-bankers is compared with market price after listing these shares. SEBI suggests new yardsticks for evaluating the quality of the merchant-banker that (1) if the issues is heavily over-subscribed, then it is a pointer to the inability of the merchant-banker to assess the situation correctly and as a result, the company is likely to be the loser in such a case (2) the percentage of issues handled by a merchant-banker which quote above par/issues price is likely to become another yardstick.

The recent trends in the new issue market in India suggest that merchant-bankers have played a very significant role through corporate sector for mobilising funds from the public. The funds raised by the companies through public issues during the year 1995-96 amounted to nearly Rs. 11822 crore, through 1428 issues compared to Rs. 1311 crore, through 1343 issues during 1944-95 and Rs. 12344 crore from 770 issues during 1993-94 and Rs. 6060 crore from 531 issues during 1992-93 and Rs. 1711 crore from 196 issues during 1991-92.

, The overall performance with regard to new issue management and underwriting in terms of number and value during the period between 1991-92 and 1994-95 of the sample lead merchant-bankers are discussed in the following paragraphs.

Overall New Issue Performance Analysis

All the sample units are undertaking the issue management services. The new issue performance of the sample merchant-bankers have included the management of different types of instruments namely equity, convertible debentures, bonds etc. The performance of the sampled merchant-bankers in this regard is given in Table 7.1. The new issue performance of the sample merchant-bankers between 1991-92 and 1994-95 reveals that the AFI, NBS performance in terms of volume and in number of issues had been constantly increasing over the years except in 1994-95 in the case of AFI. The new issue performance in terms of volume and number of the Private Merchant-bankers had been steadily increasing over the years. But some of the study units have started their new issue business during 1993-94, hence, information about the new issue business during 1991-92 and 1992-93 of those units were not available. It is concluded that even though, the private sector merchant-bankers had very limited amount of experience and finance, their performance in respect of the new issue management in terms of number and volume was commendable when compared to the Financial Institution and Bank-based merchant-bankers. However, it is difficult to compare the performance of all the sample units because of the level of operation and organisational setup.

Overall Underwriting Performance Analysis

All the sample units are undertaking the underwriting services. But it is raised on the financial strength of the study units. Underwriting Performance of the sample merchant-bankers between 1991-92 and 1994-95 is given in Table 7.2. It reveals that AFI, NB and NBS performance in terms of volume and in number of issues had been constantly increasing over

Table 7.1: New Issue Performance of Sample Units

(*Rupees in crores*)

Types of Merchant Bankers	*1991–92*		*1992–93*		*1993–94*		*1994–95*	
	No.	*Volume*	*No.*	*Volume*	*No.*	*Volume*	*No.*	*Volume*
AFI	10	198	23	286	30	3237	36	2240
SFI	NA	NA	NA	NA	5	19	10	41
NB	2	102	10	498	18	85	26	86
NBS	19	762	58	2877	60	484	42	667
PSB	2	64	4	352	13	66	29	95
PMB	7	27	26	266	91	391	255	699
TOTAL	40	1153	121	4279	217	4282	398	3828

Note: NA—Not Available

Sources: Compiled from Primary Data, *Business Today*, Feb 22-Mar 6, 1995, pp 131–137, *Business Today* Oct 22-Nov 6 1995 pp. 166-129 and *The Merchant Banking* Update July, 1996, pp. 46-62.

the years except in 1994-95 in the case of AFI, NBS and NB. The underwriting performance in terms of volume and number of the Private Merchant-bankers had been steadily increasing over the years. Some of the study units, have not participated in underwriting business, hence the information about these units were not available. Further, it shows that the merchant-bankers underwriting performance in terms of volume had been decreasing during 1994-95 when compared to the previous year. The major reasons for the decreasing trend were: the SEBI did away with the underwriting of issues in October, 1994; the sluggish primary market trend; and the cautious approach of the sample merchant-bankers.

Analysis of Issue Performance of sample merchant-bankers

The role of lead merchant-bankers in New Issues Management is assisting the issuer in deciding promoter's contributions, size of the project, means of financing for the project type(s) of instrument(s) for the issue. They advised to issue a right proportion of debt equality ratio that commensurate with the size of the company and nature of industry. He would also assist the company in launching equity shares of the company on a preferential reservation/firm allotment basis with Financial Institution & Foreign Institutional Investors and mutual funds in accordance with the capital structure finalised for the issue. He makes arrangement for appraisal of project report by Banks or Financial Institutions or Technical Consultancy Organisations. The lead merchant-banker must look that whether the purpose of the issue is likely to result in enhancement of the profitability and growth of the company and to appreciate and understand the location of the project and its advantages. The lead merchant-bankers assists the issuer in deciding the place for listing the securities and the number of listing of securities.

The above role of the lead merchant-bankers in the issue management raises many questions to the researcher. The questions are: (1) Which industries attracted the maximum number of issues? (2) What is the shareholding pattern of the issues? (3) How much of the money is raised for what purpose and it has gone into which type of project? (4) Which stock exchange has attracted the maximum number of listing?

Table 7.2: Underwriting Performance of Sample Units

(Rupees in crores)

Types of Merchant Bankers	*1991–92*		*1992–93*		*1993–94*		*1994–95*	
	No.	*Volume*	*No.*	*Volume*	*No.*	*Volume*	*No.*	*Volume*
AFI	45	37.0	57	50	56	270.0	37	58.0
SFI	NA	NA	NA	NA	6	22.0	22	57.0
NB	45	10.1	179	45	178	66.0	196	36.0
NBS	72	29.0	187	77	119	61.0	98	28.0
PSB	91	12.0	291	48	127	33.8	154	28.0
PMB	68	13.0	134	34	1136	267.9	1829	236.9
TOTAL	321	101.1	848	254	1622	720.7	2336	443.9

Note: NA –Note Available

Sources: Compiled from Primary Data, *Business Today,* Oct 23–Nov 6 1993, pp. 92-93, *Business Today,* April 22-May 6, 1995, pp. 128-135.

(5) How much reliance on equality needed by the promoter? (6) How do the lead merchant-bankers formulate the capital structure of the projects? etc. To find out the answers to the above questions, it is essential to analyse the issues handled by the lead merchant-bankers.

Hence, lead merchant-bankers who have participated in the new issues market with equity issues between April 1995 and March 1997 were considered for selecting the sample for this analysis. During the period, 26 lead merchant-bankers have participated in the 446 issues.

1. *Issues Managed by Lead Merchant-bankers*

Table 7.3 shows the number of issues managed by the lead merchant-bankers during the period between April 1995 and March 1997.

Table 7.3: Issues handled by Lead Merchant Bankers (Numberwise)

Participation	*Type of Merchant-bankers*						*Total*	*%*
	AFI	*SFI*	*NB*	*NBS*	*PSB*	*PMB*		
Single	00	1	5	14	0	280	300	67
Multiple	16	6	18	11	12	83	146	33
Total	16	7	23	25	12	363	446	–
%	3.59	1.57	5.16	5.60	2.69	81.39	–	100

It is evident from the above Table 7.3 that out of 446 issues, 300 were managed by the sample lead merchant-bankers individually. In the remaining 146 issues, 141 issues were handled by the two lead merchant-bankers in each issue. Another five were handled by more than two lead merchant-bankers in each issue. Out of the 446 issues, 363 (81%) issues were handled by 19 Private Merchant-bankers. Nationalised Banks, Nationalised Banks Subsidiary and All India Financial Institution have handled 23, 25 and 16 issues respectively. Therefore, the private merchant-bankers, nationalised banks, and nationalised bank subsidiary were leading in the new issue operation during the review period. Among the three types performance, the private merchant-bankers performance in respect of new issue management in terms of number is commendable.

2. *Sizewise Classification of Issues*

Size of issue is suggested by the lead merchant-bankers to the issuer. Before deciding the issue size, the lead merchant-banker has to take into consideration so many factors like requirement of finance to the issuer, market trend, industry type, the project cost, term loan facilities, cost of financing etc. The sizewise classification of issues managed by the sample merchant-bankers are given in Table 7.4.

Table 7.4: Sizewise Classification of Issues

Issue Size	*Types of Merchant-bankers*						*Total*	*%*
	AFI	*SFI*	*NB*	*NBS*	*PSB*	*PMB*		
Upto Rs. 3 crore	0	2	4	8	6	177	197	44.17
Rs. 3-5 crore	5	4	13	11	4	124	161	36.09
Rs. 6-20 crore	7	1	4	5	2	58	77	17.27
Rs. 21-50 crore	3	0	2	0	0	4	9	2.02
Over Rs. 50 crore	1	0	0	1	0	0	2	0.45
Total	16	7	23	25	12	363	446	–
%	3.59	1.57	5.16	05.60	2.69	81.39	–	100

It is obvious from Table 7.4 that 197 (44%) issues' size were ranged between rupees less than 1 crore and Rs. 3 crore and another 161 (36%) issues size ranged between Rs. 3 crore and Rs. 5 crore. It is concluded that 80 per cent of the issues' size below Rs. 5 crore and small sized issues hit the market under the study period. One of the reasons for more number of small issues floated during the period is the effect of SEBI directives which allowed listing on the Mumbai Stock Exchange only of companies with capital of Rs. 10 crore or above. It is concluded that the private merchant-bankers handled small sized issues.

3. *Issue Size*

New issue market remained subdued during the study period. The funds mobilised by all companies through public issues during the year 1996-97 amounted to above Rs. 11,648 crore through 753 issues' compared Rs. 11,822 crore, through 1428 issues during 1995-96 and 13,111 crore through 1343 issues during 1994-95. Therefore, number of issues hit the market and amount mobilised during 1996-97 was lesser. The issues handled by the sampled merchant-bankers in terms of number and volume is shown in the Table 7.5 and Table 7.6.

Tables 7.5 and 7.6 shows that the funds mobilised by sample merchant-bankers for companies through equity issues during the period between 1.4.95 and 31.3.96 amounted to Rs. 1722 crores through 341 issues compared to Rs. 435 crore through 105 issues during the period between 1.4.96 and 31.3.97.

Table 7.5: Issue Size (Amountwise) *(Rs. in crore)*

Particulars	*Types of Merchant-bankers*						*Total*
	AFI	*SFI*	*NB*	*NBS*	*PSB*	*PMB*	
Number of MBs	1	1	2	1	2	19	26
Total amount raised during 1995-96	402	23	124	177	35	961	1722
Average Issue size per month during 1995-96	33.50	1.92	10.33	14.75	2.42	80.10	143.02
Total amount raised during 1996-97	11	3	11	23	2	385	435
Average Issue Size per month during 1996-97	0.92	0.25	0.92	1.92	0.16	32.08	36.25
Total Amount raised during 1995-97	413	26	135	200	37	1346	2157
Average Issues Size per month during 1995-97	17.21	1.08	5.63	8.33	1.54	56.08	89.87

Total 7.5 reveals that the performance of the sample merchant-bankers in terms of volume had been constantly decreasing during the year 1996-97 when compared to previous year. During 1995-96 the performance of the PMB, AFI NBS in terms of volume of issues had been impressive.

Table 7.6 reveals that the performance of the sample merchant-bankers in terms of number have been constantly

Table 7.6: Issue Size (Numberwise)

Particulars	*Types of Merchant Bankers*						*Total*
	AFI	*SFI*	*NB*	*NBS*	*PSB*	*PMB*	
Number of MBs	1	1	2	1	2	19	26
Number of Issues during 1995-96	14	6	20	19	11	271	341
Average Number of Issues per month during 1995-96	1.16	0.5	1.67	1.58	0.92	22.58	28.42
Number of Issues during 1996-97	2	1	3	6	1	92	105
Average Number of Issues per month during 1996-97	0.17	0.08	0.25	0.50	0.08	7.67	8.75
Number of Issues during 1995-97	16	7	23	25	12	363	446
Average Number of Issues per month during 1995-97	0.67	0.29	0.96	1.04	0.50	15.13	18.58

decreasing during the year 1996-97 when compared to previous year. During 1995-96 the performance of the PMB NBS, and NB in terms of number of issues have been impressive.

During the year 1995-96 the average issue size and average number of issues per month were 143.5 crore and 28 issues respectively. During the year 1996-97 the average issue size and average number of issues per month were 36.25 crore and 9 issues respectively. The issue performance of the sample merchant-bankers in terms of number and volume has been reduced during 1996-97 and the general trend was reflected in the sample study also.

4. *Issue Type*

With no control on printing of issues, companies have enthusiastically mobilised funds through premium issues. Here the objectives of the issuer and the lead merchant are in conflict. The issuer has a greater degree of comfort if a premium is charged as the debt-equity ratio is low. It assures loans from banks or financial institutions. But for the lead merchant-banker, a higher premium would be rejected by the market and the list price could be lower than the offer price entitling a downslide risk in the short term. Therefore, the lead merchant-banker should be cautious to fix up the amount of premium and if warranted, to launch at par. Tables 7.7 and 7.8 are showing the issues type of 446 issues handled by the sampled merchant-bankers.

Table 7.7: Issue Type (Amountwise)

Issue Type	*Types of Merchant-bankers*						*Total*	*%*
	AFI	*SFI*	*NB*	*NBS*	*PSB*	*PMB*		
Premium	353	18	38	168	21	322	920	43
Par	60	8	97	32	16	1024	1237	57
Total	413	26	135	200	27	1346	2157	–
%	19.15	1.20	6.26	9.27	1.72	62.40	–	100

Table 7.8: Issue Type (Number–wise)

Issue Type	*Types of Merchant-bankers*						*Total*	*%*
	AFI	*SFI*	*NB*	*NBS*	*PSB*	*PMB*		
Premium	9	4	4	14	4	43	78	17
Par	7	3	19	11	8	320	368	83
Total	16	7	23	25	12	363	446	–
%	19.15	1.20	6.26	9.27	1.72	62.40	–	100

It is evident from Table 7.7 and 7.8 that of the 446 issues analysed, 78 were at a premium. Though the number of premium issues was just 17.49 per cent, in terms of value the figures were staggering. Of the total amount of Rs. 2157 crore raised, Rs. 920 crore (43%) was the premium component. Most of the companies charged the highest premium. The range of premium was between Rs. 5 and Rs. 150. More than 50 per cent of the issues of AFI, SFI and NBS were premium issues. But in case of private merchant-bankers 320 issues out of 363 were par issues. It is concluded that majority of the private merchant-bankers handled the par issues.

5. *Fixing Application Amount*

At the time of pricing the issues, the important work of the lead merchant-banker is to fix up the application amount.

If the application money is more, it is difficult to procure minimum subscription because the investors may not subscribe largely. If it is less, it is inconvenient to both the merchant-banker and the issuer to procure issue money from large number of investors. But at the same time, the lead merchant-banker and the issuer have considered the investor mentality and the SEBI stipulation for fixing the minimum number of share applications and application amount. Formerly SEBI fixed up that the minimum number of applications should not be less than 500, but later it was made less than 200. Further, the minimum application money to be paid shall not be less than 25 per cent of the issue price. During the study period minimum application amount was to be paid Rs. 1250 (before this SEBI's revision), and it is 500 after the SEBI's revision. Therefore, it is essential to look into the application amount fixed by the lead merchant-bankers under the study period. The application amount for 446 issues handled by the sample units are presented in Table 7.9.

Table 7.9: Application Amount

Application amount	*Types of Merchant-bankers*						*Total*	*%*
	AFI	*SFI*	*NB*	*NBS*	*PSB*	*PMB*		
Upto Rs. 1500	5	3	5	8	2	113	136	30.5
Rs. 1501 to Rs. 3000	9	4	12	8	3	154	190	42.6
Rs. 3001 to Rs. 4500	1	0	0	1	1	2	5	1.1
Rs. 4501 to Rs. 6000	1	0	6	6	6	94	113	25.3
Above Rs. 6000	0	0	0	2	0	0	2	0.5
Total	16	7	23	25	12	363	446	–
%	3.59	1.57	5.16	5.60	2.69	81.39	–	100

It is evident from Table 7.9 that out of 446 issues, application amount from 326 issues (73%) was below Rs. 3000. This might be due to the revision of the SEBI norms for minimum number of application size and the depressed primary market conditions. As the size of the issue was small, it would be natural to fix up the application money at lower level. Therefore, it is concluded that the issuer with the aid of merchant-bankers' fix the application money for the issues at a normal level and it is not at a higher level.

6. *Project Location*

Generally, there is much concentration of industrial activities in the western region of India like Mumbai, Gujarat, Indore etc. At the same time, places like Calcutta, Delhi, Chennai, Jaipur, Hyderabad have attracted the issuers to start their business because of the benefits like availability of land, raw materials, power supply, backward area benefits etc. Table 7.10 shows the location of the project and of the issues handled by the sample merchant-bankers.

Table 7.10: Project Location

Project Locations	*Types of Merchant-bankers*						*Total*	*%*
	AFI	*SFI*	*NB*	*NBS*	*PSB*	*PMB*		
Tamilnadu	2	0	1	4	3	61	71	15.92
Andhra Pradesh	3	–	9	2	–	53	67	15.02
Karnataka	1	–	4	2	–	14	21	4.71
Madhya Pradesh	1	0	1	1	1	11	15	3.36
Gujarat	2	–	2	6	–	56	66	14.80
Maharashtra	–	1	2	2	2	30	37	8.29
Rajasthan	2	–	–	2	–	16	20	4.48
Delhi	–	–	–	–	–	11	11	2.47
Uttar Pradesh	2	6	1	1	–	20	30	6.73
Haryana	1	–	–	3	–	8	12	2.69
Other states	2	0	3	1	1	23	30	6.73
Not mentioned	–	–	–	1	5	60	66	14.80
Total	16	7	23	25	12	363	446	–
%	3.59	1.57	5.16	5.60	2.69	81.39	–	100

Note: Other places includes Kerala, Orissa, Goa, Punjab, Himachal Pradesh, West Bengal, Bihar, Pondicherry, Andaman.

It is evident from Table 7.10 that Tamilnadu, Andhra Pradesh, Gujarat accounted for 71 (15.92%), 67 (15.02%) and 66 (14.80%) number of projects of the total number of projects respectively. At the same time the promoters were also having their choice to locate the projects in other places also. It is concluded that an increasing number of projects have been established in states like Tamilnadu, Andhra, Gujarat, Karnataka, Rajasthan other than the most influential, industrial location like Maharashtra, Kolkata and Delhi.

7. *Industry Allocation*

A study on which type of the industry has attracted large number of capital issues threw up some interesting data. Table 7.11 shows the industrywise classification of the issues handled by the sample merchant-bankers.

Table 7.11: Industrywise Classification

Industry	*Types of Merchant-bankers*						*Total*	*%*
	AFI	*SFI*	*NB*	*NBS*	*PSB*	*PMB*		
Agro Food Products	4	–	2	1	1	46	54	12.11
Textiles	3	–	5	5	–	25	38	8.52
Chemicals	–	4	3	5	–	58	70	15.70
Metal and metal products	3	1	1	2	–	25	32	7.17
Machinery	1	–	2	5	2	30	40	8.97
Utilities and Infrastructure	–	–	–	–	–	4	4	0.94
Miscellaneous	4	2	6	5	3	30	50	11.22
Services	1	–	4	2	6	145	158	35.43
Total	16	7	23	25	12	363	446	–
%	3.59	1.57	5.16	5.60	2.69	81.39	–	100

The service industry issued with 158 issues accounted for 35% of the total number of issues. Another core sector of industry namely chemical had 70 issues which accounted for 16 per cent of the total number of issues. Agro-food products industry issued 54 issues which accounted for 12 per cent of the total number of issues. In the service sector, out of 158 issues, 131 issues were of the Non-Banking Financial Companies (NBFCs) that came to the market during the period of the study. NBFCs have issued the largest number of issues and the majority of the NBFCs issues were managed by the private merchant-bankers. It is concluded that the service industry hit more number of issues in the primary market under the study period.

8. *Purpose of the Issue*

The purpose for which the funds can be raised have some significance. The purpose of the issue is very important for obtaining project finance from the banks and financial institutions. Therefore, the lead merchant-banker must look into the purpose of the issues at the time of accepting the new issue mandate. The Table 7.12 shows the purpose of the issue handled by the sample merchant-bankers.

Table 7.12: Purpose of the Issue (Number–wise)

Purpose	*Types of Merchant-bankers*						*Total*	*%*
	AFI	*SFI*	*NB*	*NBS*	*PSB*	*PMB*		
New Project	1	–	1	1	–	20	23	5.16
Modernisation	4	3	3	4	1	49	64	14.35
Expansions	4	4	3	9	–	76	96	21.53
Diversification	7	–	15	8	5	105	140	31.39
Working capital	–	–	–	2	2	84	88	19.73
Capital Restructuring	–	–	1	1	4	29	35	7.85
Total	16	7	23	25	12	363	446	–
%	3.59	1.57	5.16	5.60	2.69	81.39	–	100

Out of the 446 issues 140 (31.39%) issues had the diversification purpose for raising the funds. Next to diversification, expansion was the primary purpose for raising finance for 96 (21.53%) issues. The other important purposes for which funds were raised to meet working capital, modernisation, etc. It is concluded that nearly 53 per cent of the project finance was raised for the purpose of diversification and expansion. This may be one of the reasons for the development of the industrial growth.

Table 7.13 shows the purpose for which the funds mobilised by the issuers during the study period.

In terms of issue size, the purposes for diversification, expansion and modernisation accounted for 632 crore, 425 crore and 572 crore of the total amount respectively. It is concluded that the main purposes of the issue for the issuer's were diversification, expansion and modernisation.

Table 7.13: Purpose of the Issue (Amount–wise)

(Rs. in crore)

Purpose	*Types of Merchant Bankers*						*Total*	*%*
	AFI	*SFI*	*NB*	*NBS*	*PSB*	*PMB*		
New Project	30	–	1	3	–	105	139	6.43
Modernisation	229	13	11	100	4	215	572	26.52
Expansion	72	13	2	41	–	297	425	19.70
Diversification	82	–	98	36	14	402	632	29.31
Working Capital	–	–	–	8	11	236	255	11.83
Restructuring	–	–	23	12	8	91	134	6.21
Total	413	26	135	200	37	1346	2157	–
%	19.15	1.20	6.26	9.27	1.72	62.40	–	100

9. *Project Cost*

If the requirement of finance for the project is small, the issuers depend on their own contributions. On the other hand, the size of the project is a big one, and he has to depend on sources like issue of securities, loan from banks and financial institution. The lead merchant-banker should properly evaluate the source of finance apart from the evaluation of the project, so that he can suggest the public issue portion to the issuers, means of borrowing from the banks and financial institutions etc. The data on cost of projects relate to 446 issues are presented in Table 7.14.

It can be observed from Table 7.14 that out of the 446 project, 140 (31%) projects' cost ranged between Rs. 1 crore and Rs. 5 crore, and another 197 (44%) projects' cost ranged between Rs. 6 crore and Rs. 10 crore. It is concluded that the 88 per cent of the issues projects' cost were below Rs. 15 crore and the cost of the projects were normally in small size. Out of the 446 projects, only 2 projects were in mega size (i.e. Rs. 100 crore and more). Therefore, it is concluded that more number of small size projects have entered into the primary market and there were much dependence on the primary market for mobilisation of funds during the study period.

Table 7.14: Project Size (Number–wise)

Project Size	*Types of Merchant-bankers*						*Total*	*%*
	AFI	*SFI*	*NB*	*NBS*	*PSB*	*PMB*		
Rs. 1-5 crore	0	4	1	4	6	125	140	31.38
Rs. 6-10 crore	1	3	11	12	4	166	197	44.18
Rs. 11-15 crore	2	–	4	5	–	48	59	13.23
Rs. 16-20 crore	3	–	2	1	2	12	20	4.48
Rs. 21-25 crore	1	0	1	1	0	2	5	1.13
Above Rs. 25 crore	9	0	4	2	0	10	25	5.60
Total	16	7	23	25	12	363	446	–
%	3.59	1.57	5.16	5.60	2.69	81.39	–	100

Further, Table 7.15 reveals that the funds mobilised under different category of project cost by the lead merchant-bankers who have handled 446 issues.

Table 7.15: Project Size (Amount–wise)

(Rs. in crore)

Project Size–Group	*Types of Merchant-bankers*						*Total*	*%*
	AFI	*SFI*	*NB*	*NBS*	*PSB*	*PMB*		
Rs. 1-5 crore	0	13	1	10	17	256	297	13.77
Rs. 6-10 crore	4	13	34	45	13	565	677	31.39
Rs. 11-15 crore	9	–	17	24	–	252	302	14.00
Rs. 16-20 crore	21	–	7	7	7	59	97	4.5
Rs. 21-25 crore	7	–	7	14	–	20	46	2.13
Rs. 26-50 crore	27	–	18	13	–	109	167	7.74
Rs. 51-75 crore	0	0	0	0	0	40	40	1.85
Above 75 crore	345	0	51	87	0	45	531	24.62
Total	413	26	135	200	37	1346	2157	
%	19.15	1.20	6.26	9.27	1.72	62.40	–	100

Out of Rs. 2157 crore mobilised in the new issue market, 297 (13.77%) crore were mobilised under the Project Cost of Rs. 1 to 5 crore, 677 (31.39%) crore were mobilised under the Project Cost of Rs. 6 to 10 crore and another Rs. 302 (14%) crore were mobilised under the project cost of Rs. 11 to 15 crore. It is also evident from the above table that Rs. 571 (26.37%) crore were mobilised for the project cost of above Rs. 51 crore. Hence, out of Rs. 2157 crore, Rs. 1276 (58%) crore were mobilised under the project cost range between Rs. 1 crore and Rs. 15 crore. It is concluded that the private merchant-bankers handled the small size project to the issuer as their strength in the arrangement of project finance was weak.

10. Debt–Equity

The proportion of equity in the capital structure of a company is determined by debt–equity ratio stipulated by the government, restrictions imposed by financial institutions and requirements to be met for listing on stock exchanges. The debt-equity ratio stipulated on government in its guideline is 2:1. But it is not applicable in all cases. For example, capital intensive projects of higher ratios in the range of 3:1 to 6:1 have been allowed. In this case of projects located in backward areas, project initiated by techno entrepreneurs and small scale units also higher ratios are permitted. Financial institutions require that promoters contribute 22.5 per cent of the project cost and in backward areas a lower contribution of 17.5 per cent is required.

The listing requirements of the stock exchange stipulate that a company should offer 25 per cent of issued capital for public subscription. Under the capital structure, the lead merchant-bankers should take into consideration the above factors for fixing the debt-equity ratio. It is not low geared (Debt consist low portion to the capital) or high geared (Debt consist of high proportion to the capital) and it should be properly geared. The debt-equity ratio of the sample merchant-bankers who have handled the 446 issues are given in Table 7.16.

The debt-equity ratio of the companies under review shows that 38 per cent of the companies did not rely on the debt. Another 24 per cent of the companies debt-equity ratio were between 0.20 and 1.00. The normal debt-equity ratio is 2:1. But majority (56%) of the companies under review had debt position between 0.01 and 1.00. This indicates that the companies relied more on the equity than debt. Too much reliance on the equity will affect the investors interest in the

Table 7.16: Debt-Equity Ratio

Debt–equity	*Types of Merchant Bankers*						*Total*	*%*
ratio range	*AFI*	*SFI*	*NB*	*NBS*	*PSB*	*PMB*		
Upto 0.20 : 1	–	3	4	6	3	91	107	23.99
0.21-0.40 : 1	3	1	5	7	4	52	72	16.14
0.41-0.60 : 1	3	–	7	7	–	31	48	10.77
0.61-0.80 : 1	1	–	2	1	–	13	17	03.81
0.81-1.00 : 1	2	–	2	–	–	5	9	02.02
1.01-2.00 : 1	6	–	3	–	–	9	18	04.04
Above 2.01 : 1	–	–	–	–	–	6	6	01.34
Not Debt	1	3	–	4	5	156	169	37.89
Total	16	7	23	25	12	363	446	–
%	3.59	1.57	5.16	5.60	2.69	81.39	–	100

form of lesser amount of dividend payment. Another aspect is that 38 per cent of the projects are financed entirely by equity without recourse of debts. This means, either the promoters are under the misguided impression that equity is cheaper than debt or the projects have not been found credit-worthy by the lending institutions. Most of the companies find the norms for appraisal and valuation more strict and prefer to fund their projects with 100 per cent equity. This trend is harmful for manufacturing companies. For one, they get over capitalised and two there is no tax exemption on dividend payments as in the case of interest payment on debt. Therefore, it is concluded that the private merchant-bankers did not properly advised the issuers to fix up the properly geared debt-equity ratio for their project.

11. Project appraisal

The project appraisal is carried out by the entrepreneur or promoters of the project. The merchant-banker who is going to be involved in the management of public issue and underwriting it and public financial institutions, may lend money. This was practised until 1996, but as per 1996 guidelines of the SEBI, the financial institutions and scheduled commercial banks alone can provide project appraisal service. The project appraisal of the issues handled by the lead merchant-bankers under study, is given in Table 7.17.

Table 7.17: Project Appraisal

Nature of Appraisal	*Types of Merchant-bankers*						*Total*	*%*
	AFI	*SFI*	*NB*	*NBS*	*PSB*	*PMB*		
Unappraised	4	1	7	12	7	168	199	44.62
Merchant Bankers	12	6	8	5	5	12	48	10.76
Financial Institution and Banks	0	0	8	8	0	183	199	44.62
Total	16	7	23	25	12	363	446	–
%	3.59	1.57	5.16	5.60	2.69	81.39	–	100

It is interesting to note that out of 446 issues, 199 issues were unappraised, if there was no appraisal means there was no term loan component in the project and it was invariably full equity finance. If the offer is at par with fully equity finance, it will drag on the earning per share, if any, in the initial yeas. Such issues rarely appreciate upon listing and often quote below par. Further, of the 446 issues managed by lead merchant-bankers 48 issues alone were appraised by the sample units and 199 issues were appraised by the Financial Institutions, Banks, Co-operative Banks, Technical Consultancy Organisation etc. Except a few merchant-bankers, most of the Private Merchant-bankers did not undertake the project appraisals work. They relied mostly on public institution and commercial bankers for the appraisal of the project. Main reasons for selecting the banks and financial institutions as the appraiser for the project by issuer are the term loan assistance and the revised norms of SEBI. Hence, it is concluded that the merchant-bankers were lacking the project appraisal skill and they should develop the project appraisal skills in future.

12. Post-Issue Equity

The present issue size (equity) plus existing equity share capital of the enterprise put together is called the post-issue equity. In the case of first issue of existing private companies/ closely held companies make the public issue. The post-issue equity means promoters contribution plus present size of the issue. When the share of the promoter's contribution in the post-issue equity is more, it show higher level of promoter's confidence in the project. Therefore, a large percentage of post-issue equity indicates the strength of the project. If the promoter's contribution is more, the post-issue equity will also be more. If the issuers have more percentage of post-issue equity, it will reduce the burden of marketing the issues by the lead merchant-bankers. The post-issue equity size of the 446 issue managed by the sample units are given in Table 7.18.

Table 7.18: Post–issue Equity

Post–Issue Equity Group	*Types of Merchant-bankers*						*Total*	*%*
	AFI	*SFI*	*NB*	*NBS*	*PSB*	*PMB*		
Rs. 1-5 crore	2	5	3	10	9	163	192	43.05
Rs. 6-10 crore	4	2	15	13	3	167	204	45.74
Rs. 11-15 crore	4	0	3	1	0	28	36	8.08
Rs. 16-20 crore	2	0	1	1	0	3	7	1.57
Rs. 21-25 crore	1	0	0	0	0	0	1	0.22
Above Rs. 25 crore	3	0	1	0	0	2	6	1.34
Total	16	7	23	25	12	363	446	100
%	3.59	1.57	5.16	5.60	2.69	81.39	–	–

It is clear from Table 7.18 that nearly (46%) of the issues' post equity size ranged between Rs. 6 crore and Rs. 10 crore. Another 43 per cent of the issues' post-issue equity were between Rs. 1 crore and Rs. 5 crore. One of the reasons might be the small size issue were hit in the primary market. It is concluded that, post-issue equity amount of the issues handled by the sampled units were small. It is concluded that a small percentage of post-issue equity indicated the weakness of the project, sample merchant-bankers have handled the weak project and assumed that they did not advise the issuers to increase their contribution.

13. Share-holding Pattern

The analysis of the distribution of shares among the promoters, public, institutions, NRI and others, of the issues handled by the merchant-bankers are very essential, because it gives an idea that how the lead merchant-bankers utilise the preferential allotment and the marketing strategy. Share-holding Pattern of 446 companies that issued equity shares during the period April 1995 to march 1997 are presented in Table 7.19.

Table 7.19: Share-Holding Patterns

(Number-wise)

Percentage of holdings	*A*		*B*		*C*		*D*		*E*	
	No.	%	No.	%	No.	%	No.	%	No.	%
Nil	0	0	19	4	260	58	160	36	201	45
1-15	0	0	3	1	144	32	218	49	196	44
16-30	87	19.5	160	36	26	6	51	11	29	7
31-45	172	38.5	165	37	12	3	12	3	15	3
Above 45	187	42	99	22	4	1	5	1	5	1
Total	446	100.0	446	100	446	100	446	100	446	100

Note:

A refers to Promoters
B refers to Public
C refers to Institutions
D refers to Non–Resident Indians
E refers to Others

Table 7.19 reveals that of the 446 issues, 87 issues had the promoters share-holding just below 30 per cent which accounted for 20 per cent of the total issues. On the other hand, 172 (39%) issues had the promoters share-holding range between 31 per cent and 45 per cent. Therefore, majority of the issues handled by lead merchant-bankers with lesser percentage of promoters share-holdings may reduce the strength of the issue. In other words the promoters were not confident about their projects and prepared to invest more money in the projects.

The Table 7.19 reveals that the public portion of the 160 (36%) issues out of 446 issues managed by the merchant-bankers ranged between 16 per cent and 30 per cent and another 165 issues out of 446 issues managed by the lead merchant-banker ranged between 31 per cent and 45 per cent. Share-holding of public financial institutions and foreign financial institutions for the 144 issues out of 446 issues ranged between 1 per cent and 15 per cent. Similarly share-holding of Non-Resident Indian of the 218 issues out of 446 issues were between 1 per cent and 15 per cent. Apart from the above, the share-holding of others like Mutual Fund, Overseas Corporate Bodies, Banks etc. of the 196 issues out of 446 issues were between 1 per cent and 15 per cent. It is concluded from the above analysis that the share-holding of the financial institutions, NRI and mutual fund were in low percentage. Most of the financial institutions and mutual funds are under the pressure to increase their income. Hence, they are more concerned about interest and less about dividend. Therefore, the participation of the institutions, NRI and mutual fund in the new issue were very limited. This may be due to the sluggish primary market trend prevailing in the study period. Hence, it is concluded from the above study that the lead merchant-bankers have not properly utilised the preferential allotment and marketing strategy.

14. *Number of Listing*

Listing of the shares is a mandatory obligation on the part of the issuer. Moreover, it provides liquidity to the shares. The number of listing and the place of the stock exchanges are the choice of the issuer. More number of listing may provide more liquidity to the shares. Generally the Indian companies are having their first preference to list their shares in Mumbai stock exchange. But out of 7000 and odd listed shares in Mumbai stock exchange, hardly 300 shares are regularly traded. Hence mere listing in a particular stock exchange will not give trading of shares. In this connection the issuer also looks into the difficulty of cost of listing (initial listing fees and renewal fees) and timely submission of the financial statement and other particulars. Further, delisting can take place owing to several reasons, the most commonly cited being non-payment of listing fees.[1] Therefore, at the time of listing the issue the lead manager has to suggest the necessary number of listing and persuade the company to list the shares where there is a possibility of trading of shares. The information about the number of listings are presented in Table 7.20.

Table 7.20: Number of Listing

Number of Listing	*Types of Merchant-bankers*						*Total*	*%*
	AFI	*SFI*	*NB*	*NBS*	*PSB*	*PMB*		
Single	0	0	0	0	1	10	11	2
Double	1	0	9	4	3	127	144	32
Triple	6	1	8	9	5	142	171	38
Four	3	1	4	8	2	55	73	17
Above Four	6	5	2	4	1	29	47	11
Total	16	7	23	25	12	363	446	–
%	3.59	1.57	5.16	5.60	2.69	81.39	–	100

It is very interesting to note from Table 7.20 that 11 (2.47%) issues out of 446 companies issues listed their shares in a single stock exchange. More than 70 per cent of the issuers listed their shares in two to three stock exchanges. It is concluded that the issuers were willing to list the shares in more than one exchange. AFI, NBS and SFI handled issues were listed in more than three stock exchanges. Majority of the private merchant-bankers handled issues were listed in two/three stock exchanges. The reason may be the AFI, SFI and NBS issues' size were big. Hence, it may be essential to list the shares in more number of stock exchanges. It is observed from the study that either the issuers or the merchant-bankers were not confident to list their shares in a single stock exchange and listing of security in multiple stock exchanges is the order of the day.

15. *Place of listing*

At present there are 21 stock exchanges operating in India. Out of which two namely, OTCEI and NSE are screen-based stock exchanges. Stock exchanges provide liquidity, marketability and price discovery of the listed securities. Therefore, the choice of the stock exchange for listing is an important factor to the issuer. Among the stock exchanges, which has attracted the issuer more? What are the reasons behind it? The answers to the above questions are necessary. For this purpose, the information about the place of stock exchanges where the shares listed are presented in Table 7.21.

Table 7.21: Place of Listing

Place of Listing	*Types of Merchant-bankers*						*Total*	*%*
	AFI	*SFI*	*NB*	*NBS*	*PSB*	*PMB*		
Ahmedabad	7	6	10	18	6	220	267	20.15
Mumbai	10	5	21	18	8	239	301	22.72
Calcutta	5	2	3	4	0	44	58	4.38
Delhi	8	7	6	7	2	102	132	9.96
Hyderabad	3	1	15	6	3	87	115	8.68
Jaipur	3	3	1	4	3	65	79	5.96
Chennai	6	1	3	11	2	147	170	12.83
Coimbatore	1	0	0	3	1	40	45	3.39
Other Places	8	8	9	12	4	117	158	16.45
Total	51	33	68	83	29	1061	1325	–
%	3.85	2.49	5.13	6.26	2.19	80.08	–	100

Note: Other places include Bangalore, Cochin, Guwahati, Indore, Kanpur, Ludhiana, Pune, Rajkot, Bhuvaneshwar, Vadodara, Magadha, NSE and OTCEI.

It is clear from Table 7.21 that in all the 21 stock exchanges totally 1325 number of listings were made for 446 issues. Out of 1325 number of listing, Mumbai, Ahmedabad, Chennai, Delhi and Hyderabad were having 301, 267, 170, 132, 115 number of listings respectively. There was no surprise that the Premier stock exchanges namely Mumbai, Delhi, Chennai, Calcutta etc. were having more number of listing but Ahmedabad stock exchange was having 267 number of listing. This means that the companies preferred to list their shares in Ahamedabad stock exchange. In the recent past, the places like Ahmedabad and Jaipur have attracted both the issuer and the lead merchant-banker for the new issue business. During the personal interview with the merchant-bankers they opined that they used to sell major portion of share in Mumbai, Ahmedabad and Jaipur. These figures made it very important to discuss the length of survival of the companies. Because, the issuers initially listed their shares in one or more than one stock exchanges. But later on delisted due to non-payment of listing fees. Therefore, it is concluded that Mumbai and Ahmedabad have more number of listing than in other places. Apart from the above places, the places like Hyderabad, Coimbatore and Bangalore also had the attraction for listing. Further, there were concentration of listing in a few stock exchanges. It is concluded that the sample merchant-bankers have advised the issuers to list their shares in Jaipur, Ahamedabad and Mumbai, because they used to sell the shares easily in those places.

Effectiveness of Merchant Banking Services

The role of merchant-bankers, however, needs to be examined in its totality and not early in terms of number of issues and volumes managed. It would be premature to make any judgement on the performance of the merchant-bankers unless the post-issue performance of the issues managed by them is examined. In other words, an examination of the post-issue performance of companies raising funds from the primary market through the merchant-bankers is imperative for a better understanding of the role played by the merchant-bankers on the one hand and of the efficiency of the new issue markets on the other.

"A management in the service industry is concerned with the spiritual effect which they do by providing service which is their output but intangible. If the clients value the services, then only the service industry has made a spiritual effect on the clients. Therefore, the measure of effectiveness in service industry will be the value of their output, not the output itself".[2] In the case of new issue management services, the clients to the merchant-bankers are the issuers. The issuers' clients are the investors. The investors value the issuers' service through the benefit they derive from the shares after listing in the stock exchanges. Therefore, the stock exchange index will give not only the value of the investment made by the investor but also it gives the value of the service of the merchant-bankers and issuer. Hence, the present part of the chapter focuses the value of the output that is the new issues. Before going to discuss the new issue performance of the merchant-bankers it is essential to know the methodology of this part of the discussion.

For the purpose of this analysis, the number of companies who have made public issues during 1.1.96 to 30.6.96 period have been taken. The total number of equity issues during that period were 762. These issues were handled by both the sample merchant-bankers and the other merchant-bankers. For computing the market price of the issues listing of one year as published in *Investment Week* has been taken as the base. Gains or losses are computed as on the cut off period of issues after one year, and have not been annualised. Issues which at quoted issue price have been placed in a separate category as there is neither gain nor loss to the investor.

First, the overall performance of the companies who have made the public issues and the sample merchant-bankers who have handled the issues during the period under study, have been taken up for the analysis. Table 7.22 explains the issues handled by all the Merchant-bankers traded in stock exchanges.

Table 7.22: Issues Handled by All MBs Traded in Stock Exchanges

Method of Issue	*Traded*		*Not Traded*		*Total*	
	Number	*to % Total*	*Number*	*to % Total*	*Number*	*%*
Par Issues	517	82	116	18	633	100
Premium Issues	108	85	019	15	127	100
Total	625		135		760	

Out of 762 issues, for 2 issues money was refunded, of the balance 760 issues, 135 issues were not traded in any stock exchange. The remaining 625 issues were traded in the stock exchanges. Out of the 625 shares traded, 517 were par issues and 108 were premium issues.

Of the 760 issues that hit the market, 633 were offered at par and 127 at premium issues. Out of 633 par equity issues, 517 issues were traded in the stock exchanges and of the 127 premium issues, 108 were traded in the stock exchanges. The overall performance in premium and par equity issues, which were traded in the stock exchanges are given in Table 7.23.

Table 7.23: Overall Performance in Par and Premium Equity Issues

Performance	*Par Issue*		*Premium Issue*	
	Number	*%*	*Number*	*%*
Loss	314	61	63	58
No Loss or No Gain	044	09	07	07
Gain	159	30	38	35
Total	517	100	108	100

Of the 517 par issues listed, 159 (30%) were quoted above the issues' prices, 314 (61%) quoted below; and 44 were quoted at the issue price without gain or loss. Thus, only 30 per cent of the issues have yielded gains to the investors at the current price. The above figures are illustrated in Table 7.23.

A further look into Table 7.23 reveals that about 58 per cent of the premium issues were quoted below the issue price while 35 per cent of premium issues quoted above the issue price. Thus, only 35 per cent of the premium issues have yielded gains to the investors at the current market price.

Of the 762 issues, 176 par issues and 28 premium issues were handled by the sample merchant-bankers under the study. The main purpose of this chapter is to analyse the performance of the sampled merchant-bankers who have handled issues during the above said period. Therefore, 28 premium issues and 176 par issues which were handled by the sample merchant-bankers were considered for the analysis.

The essential part of this analysis is to assess the performance of the sample lead merchant-bankers on pricing front. Because the merchant-bankers have twin responsibilities namely giving the maximum return to the investors and at the same time pricing the issue closer to the market level. Hence, the details about the sample merchant-bankers on the issue performance are prepared. It is presented in Table 7.24.

Table 7.24: Issues Handled by Sample MBs Traded in Stock Exchanges

Method of Issue	*Traded*		*Not Traded*		*Total*	
	Number	*to % Total*	*Number*	*to % Total*	Number	%
Par Issues	150	85	26	15	176	100
Premium Issues	025	089	03	11	28	100
Total	175		29		204	

Table 7.24 reveal that out of the issues handled by the lead merchant-bankers under study, 176 were par issues and 28 were premium issues. Out of the 176 par issues 26 were not quoted and out of 28 premium issues 3 were not quoted. Table 7.25 reveals that out of the 176 par issues 43 were quoted above issue price; 94 were quoted below the issue price; and 13 were quoted at the issue price without gains or loss. Thus 24 per cent of the par issues have yielded gain to the investors at the current price. Of the 28 issues, 3 issues were not traded in the stock exchanges; 16 were quoted below the issue price; 7 were quoted above the issue price; and 2 were quoted at the issues price with no gain or loss. A further look into the premium issue revealed that 7 (25%) premium issues out of 28 were quoted above issue price whole 16 (57%) of the premium issues quoted below the issue price.

In both cases (Par and Premium), in more than 68% of the issues, the investors have suffered losses. The losses were more in premium issues than in par issues. It is interesting and surprising that our study results confirmed with the survey conducted by the Trinity Live Media for Quarterly Money Managers on 428 premium issues that hit the market during 1994-95. The survey result is: "Of the 428 premium issues covered in this survey, as many as 55 per cent (235) are currently quoting below their issue prices."[3] Even though the present study sample size is minuscule, it aptly confirms with the larger sample. Therefore, there is no prudent pricing technique used by merchant-bankers under study. In this respect all the segment of the merchant-bankers are one and the same. But one thing here to remain, the Bombay stock exchange Sensex is generally on a steadily downward slope during the study period, probably the fact is that 43 per cent of the premium issues are still quoting above the issue price.

A scrutiny of Table 7.25 revealed that out of the 176 par issues 162 issues were handled by the private merchant-bankers; 8 were handled by Nationalised banks and AFI, SFI and NBS handled each 2 issues. Thus, 54 per cent of the par issues of the merchant-bankers were quoting below issue price and only 24 per cent of the issues were quoting above the issue price. A further look into Table 7.25 reveals that except AFI, all other segments of lead merchant-bankers who have handled the issues, were not quoted in the stock exchange after one year of listing.

A closer look into Table 7.25 indicates that out of 28 premium issues 19 issues were handled by the private merchant bunkers. Among the private merchant-bankers, the Prudential Capital Markets and Doogar and associates were the leaders. Among the other segments Ind Bank merchant banking division had the large number of premium issues.

There is a general belief that the issues handled by the public sector lead merchant-bankers like AFI, SFI Nationalised Banks and nationalised Bank Subsidiaries are of good quality. Hence to verify the above belief and to know the association between the performance of the Private Sectors Merchant-bankers who have handled issues with the performance of the Public sector Merchant-bankers who have handled the issues during the period from 1.1.96 to 30.6.96, an analysis has been carried out. For this purpose the sample merchant-bankers are grouped into two group, namely private sector merchant-bankers and public sector merchant-bankers.

The correlation coefficient between Issue Price (IP) and Market Price (MP) of above two group of merchant-bankers and the t–test results of the same are given in Table 7.26.

Table 7.25: Sample Merchant Bankers Performance in Par and Premium Equity issues

Performance	*Par issue Merchant Banker Group*								*Premium Issue Merchant Banker Group*							
	AFI	*SFI*	*NB*	*NBS*	*PSB*	*PMB*	*Total*	*% to Total*	*AFI*	*SFI*	*NB*	*NBS*	*PSB*	*PMB*	*Total*	*% to Total*
Traded																
Loss	2	–	3	–	–	89	94	54	1	1	1	2	–	11	16	57
No Loss No Gain	–	–	–	–	–	13	13	7	–	–	–	–	–	2	2	7
Gain	–	–	3	1	–	39	43	24	1	–	–	2	–	4	7	25
Sub-total	2	–	6	1	–	141	150	85	2	1	1	4	–	17	25	89
Not Traded	–	2	2	1	–	21	26	15	–	–	–	1	–	2	3	11
Grand Total	2	2	8	2	–	162	176	100	2	1	1	5	–	19	28	100

Table 7.26: Correlation Coefficient Results

Group	*Values*			*d.f. at*	*Results*
	r	*t*	*critical*	*0.01 level*	
Public Sector Merchant-bankers	0.90	5.507	3.707	06	High Positive Correlation Significance
Private Sector Merchant-bankers	–0.18	0.708	2.947	15	Low Negative Correlation No Significance

The correlation of IP and MP in the case of public sector merchant-bankers was highly positive but for the private sector merchant-bankers IP and MP had the very low correlation negative correlation value (–0.18). It is very clear that the association between IP and MP of the public sector merchant-bankers who have handled the issues had been significant and it construed that the public sector merchant-bankers discarded the issue mandate which came from the weak promoters. This sets the stage for rigorous evaluation of private sector lead merchant-bankers performance in different angles. That is the association between the performance of the issues handled by the public sector merchant-bankers with the performance of the issues handled by the private sector merchant-bankers. For this purpose the student t–test is applied to test the difference between the mean values. The results of the above analysis is presented in Table 7.27.

Table 7.27: t–test Results for Hypothesis

Relationship between	*Values*		*d.f. at*	*Results*
	t	*critical*	*0.01 level*	
Public Sector Merchant-bankers with Private Sector Merchant-bankers	0.054	2.807	23	No Significance

Since the difference between the 2 sample means lies inside the acceptance region, the null hypothesis is accepted and hence it is concluded that the private sector merchant-bankers' performance was not significantly different from that of public sector merchant-bankers' performance.

To substantiate the conclusion further, it is worthwhile to quote the study conducted by T.P. Madhusoodhnan and M. Thiripalraju on the performance of the merchant-bankers. In that, study, they have selected top 12 merchant-bankers in terms of number of issues handled and also the average performance of all merchant-bankers who handled only one issue each during the past four years. The study show the result as follows; "The comparison between overall performance and the performance of issues handled by different merchant-bankers indicates that performance was not significantly different except in two cases. This indicates that, in general no merchant-bankers have shown exceptional capabilities in pricing IPOs."[4] Therefore, it is finally concluded that, the lead merchant-bankers understudy did not show any serious concern for the protection of the investors interest.

REFERENCES

1. M. Thiripal Raju and Harish Maudhavan, Delisting of Companies—A total loss to the investors, *The Merchant-bankers Update,* May 1997, p. 46.
2. S. Bhattacharya, Management Effectiveness, Oxford and IBH Publishing Company, New Delhi, 1983, p. 7.
3. V.S. Fernando, "Stars of an Average Show", *The Quarterly Money Managers, Business Standard,* Aug–Oct., 1995, p. 85.
4. T.P. Madhusoodanan and M. Thirupalraju, Under Pricing in Initial Public Offerings, The Indian Evidence, *Vikalpa* Vol. 22 No. 4, Oct–Dec 1997, pp. 24–25.

8

Findings, Conclusion and Suggestions

Based on the foregoing analysis, the following broad findings and conclusions have been arrived at, which are presented in this Chapter. A few recommendations have also been made, as measures for improving the way of functioning of the merchant-bankers and the quality of the new issue.

New issue management services usually entail the management of new issues on behalf of corporate clients or institutions, the origination, underwriting and distribution and all other administrative work in connection with the new issues. It involves varied functions. It starts with designing up the capital structure, type of issue instrument, preparing draft prospectus, complying with the various legal requirements, finalising the marketing strategy and ends with the mobilisation of funds from the investors. To perform the above functions, some specialised skills are needed. The company promoter may not perform the new issue management function individually and make the issue a success. The promoter must depend on so many new issue management agencies like merchant-bankers, underwriter, share broker, issue houses and print media. In new issue markets, a merchant-banker is one of the many important agencies employed by the company to assist in mobilisation of funds. However, there is a critical difference between the merchant-banker and other agencies. He selects and co-ordinates the other agencies. In the new issue process, merchant-banker has to shoulder a major responsibility and be indirectly responsible for the acts of other agencies. Therefore, this study on the functioning of merchant banking in new issue management services significance.

The scope of the present study focused on the new issue management services of merchant-bankers in all the zones of the country, comprising of Tamilnadu, Andhra Pradesh, Maharashtra, Delhi, Kerala, West Bengal and Uttar Pradesh. This study embraced a period of 5 years i.e. from 1992-93 to 1996–97 and Primary data the period concentrated on two financial years namely 1995-96 and 1996-97.

The broad objectives of the present study are outlined as under: (1) to identify the functional activities of issue management and n^w issue management services undertaken by the merchant-bankers. (2) to study the organisational structure and general profile of the merchant-bankers. (3) to assess the functioning of the merchant-bankers in the pre-issue and post-issue management phases. (4) to evaluate the new issue performance of the merchant-bankers. (5) to examine the reactions of the lead merchant-bankers towards the measures of the SEBI and Stock Exchanges.

In connection with the above objectives some hypotheses were framed and verified during the course of the study. A sample of 26 merchant-bankers in all the zones of the country was covered for a detailed study. Secondary data were collected from published materials. The primary data were used to study general profile of merchant-bankers, analyse the pre-issue and post-issue management functions, the impact of authorities' measures and analyse the new issue performance of the sampled merchant-bankers. The secondary data were used for studying the regulatory framework in the new issue management. Statistical techniques were used to analyse the data collected. The profile of the new issue market and merchant banking industry were also explained.

MAJOR FINDINGS

Merchant-bankers—General Profile

1. Majority of the (21) sample units have been doing banking and stock broking activities, but merchant banking activity began from 1993 onwards.

2. During the year 1992-93 alone, 19 out of 26 study units obtained authorisation from the SEBI.
3. All the study units had the computers and printers. Some of the merchant-bankers had more than required number of computers. Eleven units had E-mail and Internet facilities and twenty-four merchant-bankers had fax facilities.
4. The sampled merchant-bankers were having their branch offices mainly in Mumbai but at the same time they were having their branch offices in other places also.
5. The Private Merchant-bankers were utilising all the investors and they relied more on the corporate bodies. The banks and financial institution were having financial backing.
6. Most of the merchant-bankers were having membership in the stock exchanges in different places. Among the stock exchanges the OTCEI and NSE have accommodated more number of the study units.
7. Out of 26 study units, 20 units had membership in the Association of Merchant-bankers in India. Only 2 units had, dual membership in two Associations. The four merchant-bankers were not member in any of the associations.
8. All the private merchant-bankers depended on the services of the broker, sub-broker and underwriter for the success of the issue. The Nationalised Bankers and Private Sector Banks and State Financial Institution did not depend on them.
9. The majority of the brokers/sub-brokers and underwriters were located at major cities namely Mumbai, Chennai, Delhi, Hyderabad. The reason behind this was the merchant banking head offices or branch offices were situated in those places.
10. Out of the total 26 merchant-bankers only 11 were conducting research. Among the 11, 8 were the

private merchant-bankers and the remaining included All India Financial Institution, Nationalised Bank and Nationalised Bank Subsidiary one each.

11. Private Sector Merchant Banks and Nationalised Banks Subsidiaries were functioning as refund bankers and collecting bankers. Most of the private merchant-bankers' parent/sister concern were acting as a non-banking financial companies.
12. Out of the 26 Merchant Banking units, the principal officers of 9 units were having professional qualifications, 6 were having post-graduation as well as professional qualifications.
13. Most of the private merchant-bankers used the designation of the principal officer as Vice-President or General Manager.
14. The age of principal officers of the sampled units was in the range between 30 to 50 years. Out of the 26 merchant banking units, the 11 officers were under the age group of 30 to 40 years.
15. Twenty out of 26 merchant banking units' principal officers were having less than 10 years experience.
16. Nineteen out of twenty-six, principal officers of the different merchant banking units were getting a monthly salary ranging from Rs. 10,000 to Rs. 20,000. Another 6 principal officers got more than Rs. 20,000 as their monthly salary.
17. Nine out of 26, merchant banking units' principal officers alone have attended the special courses on merchant banking.
18. Most of the private merchant banking outfits had lesser number of employees in managerial, supervisory and operative categories.

Analysis—I Pre-Issue Management

1. The best source to acquire new issue mandate was to approach the issuer directly. The corporate client as well as advisor had some influence on deciding the merchant-banker for the proposed issue.

2. Out of 26 lead merchant-bankers 11 imposed a condition that their parent or sister concern would be one of the supporting service organisations.
3. Most of the issuers demanded that the project finance should be arranged by the merchant-banker. Another important stipulation of the issuer to the merchant-banker was the issue should be at minimum cost.
4. The nationalised banks and financial institutions were concentrating only on specific industries. There was no concentration on particular line of industries in the case of private merchant-bankers.
5. The sample merchant-bankers did not get any fees for 35 out of 148 issues. For another 83 out of 148 issues handled by them, the sample merchant-bankers charged fees below 1.00 per cent of the issue size.
6. Nine sampled units out of 26 units alone made frequent visits to the issuer project or premises.
7. Fifty per cent of the respondents felt that they needed 30-50 days for the documentation activities. But 30 per cent of the respondents felt that they needed more than 50 days, it was due to volume of information expected from the issuers.
8. Sixty-nine per cent of sample units preferred to get the project appraised by the Financial Institutions. Next to the Financial Institutions' appraisal, they preferred appraisal by both financial institutions and banks.
9. Sixty-five per cent of the respondents have agreed that the arrangement of the project finance was essential for the success of the issue.
10. Fifty per cent of the respondents have agreed that the issuer reserved the vital facts and it was very difficult to the merchant-bankers to approach the necessary source to get the valid information.
11. The majority of the respondents (69%) felt that there was a delay in getting the information in the ROC's office. This was due to the inadequate infrastructure

facilities and under-staff in the offices of the ROC in the different regions.

12. Of the 26 merchant-bankers under study 8 opined that the documentation consumed more time. Another 8 merchant bankers felt that the preparation of the draft prospectus consumed much time.

13. Sixty-two per cent of the respondents held the view that right to vetting of offer document was absolutely essential for the issue process.

14. Majority of the merchant-bankers felt that the new empowerment to vet the prospectus by lead merchant-banker was a welcomeable one and it gave better transparency in the offer documents.

15. Nine out of 26 merchant-bankers felt that they influenced the issuer to select the intermediary based on the quality of the work done on the previous occasion.

16. Twenty-two out of 26 respondents agreed that there was delay in issuing the acknowledgement card and observation letter by SEBI. This was one of the reasons for giving the vetting right to the merchant-bankers by the SEBI.

17. Of the 26 merchant-bankers 8 respondents agreed that there was a delay in ROC's office in clearance in public issue. At the same time 10 out of 26 expressed their views that there was no delay in the ROC's office.

18. Of the 26 merchant-bankers, 14 have expressed that they preferred to fix up the issue price below the market price and 8 expressed that they preferred to price their product above the market price.

19. No single factor was responsible to fix up the premium on the share. It was a combination of so many factors. Promoter track record, fundamentals of the company, industry type and earning per share were the four important factors which had influence on the fixing up of the premium on the shares.

20. The majority (62%) of the respondents were under the impression that the broker's marketing support was inadequate in the marketing of the new issue. Again 77 per cent of the respondents opined that the brokers had the low level of procurement ability. There was a mismatch between the target and actual performance.
21. Majority of the respondents (73%) agreed that the firm and preferential allotment were basic for the success of the new issue and it would promote the new issue business.
22. Eighty-five per cent of the lead merchant-bankers held the view that the safety net scheme was definitely improving the new issue market. But most of the merchant-bankers have practised buy back arrangement unofficially with the lenders and financier and not with the investors.
23. Out of the 26 merchant-bankers, 17 (65%) preferred to select the print media for their new issue advertisement. But the AFI, SFI and NBS preferred both the print media and electronic media as the size of their issue was normally big.
24. Six of the respondents (33%) felt that SEBI's decision on one year validity period for public issue would not be useful. But the majority of the respondents (77%) felt that the decision of the SEBI was definitely giving breathing time to both the issuer and merchant-bankers.
25. The market trend was a very important reason for fixing up the timing of issue. Apart from the market trend the reasons like investor's mentality, forth coming number of issues and number of mega issues on the card were also having equal bearing on the decision of the timing of the issue.
26. In majority (54%) of the units, the time lag was for a period of 30 to 89 days spell from the issue open date to acknowledgment card date for fixing the date of issue.

27. Sixty-nine per-cent of the lead merchant-bankers felt that printers did not strictly follow the time schedule. There was some delay in reaching the issue materials to various intermediaries.

Analysis—II Post-Issue Management

1. Seventeen (66%) out of 26 sample respondents, strongly agreed that the collecting banker took much time to send the collection report to the issuer. The delay was particularly high in the month of March.
2. Sixteen out of 26 (62%) merchant-bankers agreed that the report received from the collecting banker to issue was inadequate.
3. Sixty-two per cent of the respondents have agreed that collecting bankers to the issue acquired the application money after the closure of the issue.
4. Nearly 69 per cent of the respondents have strongly agreed that the Bankers to the issue took much time to reconcile the accounts.
5. Out of 26 respondents, 21 (85%) have firmly agreed that the stock exchange stipulation on allotment of shares within 30 days was absolutely essential and very useful.
6. The most of the merchant-bankers (69%) disagreed that the registrars to the issue were not co-operative with the merchant-bankers.
7 The majority of the merchant-bankers confirmed that the registrars did not allot shares on the promoter's will and followed the SEBI's guidelines and consulted the merchant-bankers in the allotment of shares.
8. Almost 73 per cent of the respondents felt that the registrars were not having adequate infrastructure and technical upgradation.
9. Thirteen out of 26 (50%) were disagreeing that the registrar did the allotment and refund orders work in a delayed manner.
10. Eighty-nine per cent of the respondents agreed that the number of listing should be based on the issue size.

11. Of the 26 merchant-bankers, 11 opined that the new measures (minimum 5 shareholders per lakh) of the stock exchange was not useful.
12. Majority of the respondents opined that the stipulation of the BSE (i.e. minimum of Rs. 10 crore for listing in BSE) was welcomeable one. Eleven out of 26 have differed from the above opinion and they stated that it was not much useful.
13. More than 50 per cent of the respondents have agreed that there was delay in settlement of claims by the issuer towards the intermediaries.
14. Twenty-three per cent of the merchant-bankers did not get their fees in due time and another 12 per cent of them did get their fees in time but not as per the agreement made with the issuer earlier.

Impact of SEBI Measures

1. The majority of the respondents under this study agreed that the registration and renewal fees were normal. But most of the merchant-bankers opined that the SEBI should give some grace time to remit the renewal fees and should intimate the expiry time or the renewal time to the merchant-bankers.
2. The performance of the lead merchant-bankers who had handled the issues multiply did not differ significantly from those who had handled issues solely.
3. Majority (73%) of the merchant-bankers agreed that there should be some reduction in the number of merchant-bankers in the industry. They also welcomed the recent measures of SEBI in making all categories of merchant-bankers as one.
4. Twenty-three out of 26 merchant-bankers accepted the inspection move of the SEBI.
5. Almost all the respondents (88%) had the opinion that SEBI's stipulation on three years track record of dividend payment was essential for the quality of issues.

6. The performance of the merchant-bankers who have handled the issues after the SEBI's norms i.e. three year track record of dividend payment did not significantly differ from those who have handled issues before such entry norms of SEBI.
7. Only 54 per cent of the respondents had the feeling that the reduction of the lock–in–period as well as the promoters contribution were very useful to promote the new issue business.
8. Out of 26 merchant-bankers under study, 19 private merchant-bankers opined that the total estimated cost of public issue might be around 15 per cent.
9. The lead merchant-bankers opined that there were differences in actual and estimated cost. The actual public issue cost was more than the cost mentioned in the offer document.
10. Eighty-one per cent of the lead merchant-bankers held the view that the stock exchange prescribed existing public issue cost percentage in respect of non-mandatory cost was not adequate and needed revision.
11. Eleven out of 26 (42 per cent) of the respondents felt that the mandatory underwriting was needed for the success of the issue.
12. Ninety-two per cent of the respondents have strongly agreed that the broking community and underwriters were not ready to accept the devolvement of the issue.
13. Nearly 50 per cent of the respondents had the opinion that there was no need to further reduction of the collection centre.
14. Twenty-three out of 26 respondents strongly agreed that the SEBI's decision on promoters procuring subscription from their association within 60 days of the closure of the issue was very useful.
15. Only 5 merchant-bankers out of 26 confirmed that there was some delay in the stock exchanges to approve the allotment.

16. Among the other reasons for the success of the issue, the two primary factors which had stronger influence on the success of the issue, were brokers network and company track record.
17. Only 9 respondents out of 26 have agreed that frequent changes in SEBI's norms spoiled the primary market.
18. There has been six basic reasons for sluggishness in the primary market. Among the six reasons the highest score achieved reason was the dud issues in the past. In this case, the entire blame did not go to the issuer, as the merchant-bankers were also partly responsible for it.

Merchant Bankers—Performance Analysis

1. The private sector merchant-bankers had very limited amount of experience and finance, their performance in respect of the new issue management in terms of number and volume was commendable when compared to the Financial Institution and Bank-based merchant-bankers.
2. The majority of the merchant-bankers underwriting performance had been decreasing during 1994-95 when compared to the previous year. The major reasons for the decreasing trend were: the SEBI did away with the underwriting of issues in October, 1994; the sluggish primary market trend; and the cautious approach of the sampled merchant-bankers.
3. Out of the 446 issues, 363 (81%) issues were handled by 19 Private Merchant-bankers. Nationalised Banks, Nationalised Bank's Subsidiary and All India Financial Institution have handled 25, 23, and 16 issues respectively. Therefore, the private merchant-bankers, nationalised banks, and nationalised bank subsidiary were leading in the new issue operation during the review period.
4. Eighty-eight per cent of the issues' size were below Rs. 5 crore and small sized issues hit the market under the study period. One of the reasons for more

number of small issues floated during the period was the anticipated SEBI directives to allow listing on the Mumbai stock exchange only of companies with capital of Rs. 10 crore or above.

5. The performancc of the sample merchant-bankers in terms of volume had been constantly decreasing during the year 1996-97 when compared to previous year. During 1995-96 the performance of the AFI, NBS in terms of volume of issues had been impressive.

6. During the year 1995-96 the average number of issues per month in terms of size and number were 143.5 crore and 28 issues respectively. During the year 1996-97 the average number of issues per month in terms of size and number were 36.25 crore and 9 issues respectively. The issue performance of the sample merchant-bankers in terms of number and volume has been reduced during 1996-97 and the general trend was reflected in the sample study also.

7. Of the 446 issues analysed 78 were at a premium. Though the number of premium issues was just 17.49 per cent, in terms of value the figures were staggering. Of the total amount of Rs. 2157 crore raised, Rs. 920 crore (43 per cent) was the premium component. Most of the companies charged the highest premium. The range of premium was between Rs. 5 and Rs. 150.

8. Out of 446 issues, 326 (73%) issues application amount were below Rs. 3000. This might be due to the revision of the SEBI norms for minimum number of application size and the depressed primary market conditions. As the size of the issue was small, it would be natural to fix up the application money at lower level.

9. Tamilnadu, Andhra Pradesh, Gujarat accounted for 71 (15.92%), 67 (15.02%) and 66 (14.70%) number of projects of the total number of projects respectively. At the same time the promoters were also having

their choice to locate the projects in other places also.

10. The service industry issued 158 issues accounted for 35 per cent of the total number so issues. Another core sector of industry namely chemicals issued 70 issues which accounted for 16 per cent of the total number of issues. In the service sector, out of 158 issues 131 issues were of the Non–Banking Financial Companies (NBFCs) that came to the market during the period under review.
11. In terms of number nearly 53 per cent of the project finance was raised for the purpose of diversification and expansion. This may be one of the reasons for the development of the industrial growth.
12. In terms of issue size, the purposes for diversification, expansion and modernisation accounted for 632 crore 425 crore and 572 crore of the total amount respectively.
13. Eighty-eight per cent of the issues project cost were below Rs. 15 crore and the cost of the projects were normally in small size. Out of the 446 projects, only 2 projects were in meagre size (i.e. Rs. 100 crores and more). Therefore, it is concluded that more number of small size projects have entered into the primary market.
14. Out of Rs. 2157 crores mobilised in the new issue market, 297 (13.77%) crore were mobilised under the Project Cost range of Rs. 1 to 5 crore, 677 (31.39%) crore were mobilised under the Project Cost range of Rs. 6 to 10 crore and another Rs. 302 (14%) crore were mobilised under the Project Cost range of Rs. 11 to 15 crore.
15. The normal debt equity ratio is 2:1. But majority (56%) of the companies under review had debt-equity position between 0.01 and 1.00. This indicates that the companies relied more on the equity than debt.
16. Of the 446 issues, 199 issues were unappraised. If there was no appraisal, it meant that there was no

term loan component in the project and it was invariably full equity finance. Further, 48 issues alone were appraised by the sampled units and 199 issues were appraised by the financial institutions, banks, Co-operative banks, Technical consultancy organisation etc.

17. Nearly 46 per cent of the issues' post-equity size ranged between Rs. 6 crores and Rs. 10 crore. Another 43 per cent of the issues' post-issue, equity ranged between Rs. 1 crore and Rs. 5 crore.

18. Out of 446 issues managed by the lead merchant-bankers, 160 (36%) of the issues public portion ranged between 16 per cent and 30 per cent and another 165 issues out of 446 issues managed by the lead merchant-banker ranged between 31 per cent and 45 per cent. Share-holding of public financial institutions and foreign financial institutions for the 144 issues out of 446 issues ranged between 1 per cent and 15 per cent. Therefore, the participation of the institutions, NRI and mutual fund in the new issue was very limited.

19. Eleven (2.47%) issues out of 446 companies issues listed their shares in a single stock exchange. More than 70 per cent of the issuers listed their shares in two to three stock exchanges. It is concluded that the issuers were willing to list the shares in more than one exchange.

20. Out of 1325 number of listing, Mumbai, Ahmedabad, Chennai, Delhi and Hyderabad were having 301, 267, 170, 132, 115 number of listings respectively. Mumbai and Ahmedabad have more number of listing than in other places. Apart from the above places, the places like Hyderabad, Coimbatore and Bangalore also had the attraction for listing. Further, there were concentration of listing in a few stock exchanges.

21. Of the 760 issues that hit the market, 633 (82%) were offered at par and nearly 18 per cent of them were

premium issues. Out of 633 par equity issues, 517 issues were traded in the stock exchanges and of the 127 premium issues, 108 were traded in the stock exchanges.

22. Of the 517 par issues listed, 159 (31%) were quoted above the issues prices; 314 (61%) were below; and 44 were quoted at the issue price without any gain or loss. Thus, only 30 per cent of the issues have yielded gains to the investors at the current price.

23. Of the issues handled by the merchant-bankers 176 issues were par and 28 were premium issues. Out of the 176 par issues 26 were not quoted; 43 were quoted above the issue price; 94 were quoted below the issue price; and 13 were quoted at the issue price without any gain or loss. Thus, only 29 per cent of the par issues have yielded gains to the investors at the current price. Of the 28 premium issues, 3 issues were not traded in the stock exchanges; 16 were quoting below the issùe price; 7 were quoting above the issue price; and 2 were quoting at the issue price with no gain or loss. A further look into the premium issues revealed that 7 (25%) premium issues out of 28 were quoting above the issue price while 16 (64%) of the premium issues quoted below the issue price. In both cases (Par and Premium), in more than 62% of the issues, the investors have suffered losses. The losses were more in premium issues than in par issues.

24. The correlation of Issue Price (IP) and Market Price (MP) in the case of public sector merchant-bankers was highly positive (0.90). The private sector merchant-bankers' IP and MP had low negative correlation value (–0.18).

25. The private sector merchant-bankers' performance was not significantly different from that of public sector merchant-bankers' performance.

CONCLUSIONS

In the light of the major findings of the study, the following conclusions have been drawn:

The new issue management service has witnessed an exploding growth till 1996. During the recent past, the new issue activities have drastically been reduced. This phenomenon might be due to the sluggish primary market and the drastic measures taken by the SEBI to control primary market. The major reasons for the growth of merchant banking in India were the establishment of SEBI and enactment of separate rules and regulations for merchant-bankers.

The development of merchant banking requires adequate amount of infrastructure and constant research. But the study disclosed that the merchant-bankers did not pay much attention to the research. Further, the training facilities for the merchant-bankers are inadequate and lesser number of staff members have been attending the special training courses. There were insufficient operative and supervisory staff members in the existing merchant banking units and the managerial staff members were having less experience. The salary paid to them were not commensurate with their experience.

The lead merchant-bankers did not concentrate on a particular line of industry. It was regular practice of merchant-bankers to make arrangement of project finance and bridge finance. For above purpose, they preferred to get the project appraised from the financial institutions. It was also practice of some of the merchant-bankers not to get any service charges. Further, there was delay in settlement of claims by the issuer to the intermediaries.

As far as the preparation of disclosure was concerned, the lead merchant-banker found it difficult to gather information from ROCs and issuers. The major reason for allowing the merchant-bankers to vet the prospectus was the delay in issuing acknowledgement card/observation letter by SEBI. Promoters background, fundamentals, industry type and EPS had major influence in fixing up of premium on the shares.

The safety net scheme was definitely reviving and improving the new issue market. The marketing support and procurement ability of the brokers were inadequate. It was the practice of the collecting banker to accept the collection money after the closure of the issue. They also took much time not only to send the collection report but also to reconcile the accounts.

The registrars' office were not having adequate amount of infrastructure and technical upgradation. The merchant-bankers did not depend on the public investor for new issue business. The service industry issued more number of issues during the study period. The primary reasons for mobilising funds are diversification and expansion. During the study period 50 per cent of the issues were unappraised. The merchant-bankers were lacking the project appraisal skill and it should be developed in future. The issues had the low level of debt-equity ratio and it indicated that companies relied more on the equity than debt.

The preferential allotment was not properly utilised by the merchant-bankers. Majority of the issues was listed in two or more stock exchanges. Among the stock exchanges, Mumbai and Ahmedabad had more number of listing than in other stock exchanges. The investors had suffered losses more in premium than in par issues.

In the post–issue performance, the performance of private sector merchant-bankers' was not significantly different from that of public sector merchant-bankers' performance. Similarly, the performance of merchant-bankers who had handled the issues multiple did not differ significantly from those who hand handled issues solely.

Majority of the merchant-bankers welcomed the following measures of SEBI for regulating the new issue market:

1. Abolition of the category of merchant-bankers.
2. Three years track record of dividend payment.
3. Allotment of shares within 30 days.
4. Minimum of Rs. 10 crore for listing in BSE.
5. One year validity period for the issue opening. The percentage of non-mandatory cost should be revised.

Among other factors, the brokers network and company track record had stronger influence on the success of the issue. The major reason for the sluggish primary market was the dud issues in the past. The underwriting performance of the lead merchant-bankers was not good and this may be due to the scrapping of mandatory underwriting requirements of SEBI. The private merchant-bankers fixed the application amount at normal level and they handled mostly the par issues. Further, they handled small size project for the issuer as their strength in the arrangement of project finance was weak.

Therefore, it is finally concluded that, the lead merchant-bankers understudy did not show any serious concern for the protection of the investors interest.

SUGGESTIONS TO IMPROVE NEW ISSUE MANAGEMENT BY MERCHANT-BANKERS

Pre-Issue Management

1. Merchant-bankers may concentrate on a particular line of industry, which will enable them to manage the quality issue.
2. The merchant-bankers may make frequent visits to the project site.
3. The authorities may take necessary steps to increase the infrastructure facilities in the Registrar of Companies' office and to increase the staff members adequately.
4. The Private merchant-bankers are unable to provide project finance to issuers as they are restricted to perform the fund-based activities by SEBI. Hence, it is suggested that private merchant-bankers may be permitted to undertake fund-based activities like the financial institutions and banks-based merchant-bankers.
5. Safety Net Scheme was practised by only few merchant-bankers. Therefore, it is suggested that the SEBI may make the Safety Net Scheme mandatory for all public issues.
6. It is suggested that merchant-bankers may on their own dispatch the issue materials with the aid of courier services and not entirely depend on the printers for this services.

7. It is recommended that the merchant-bankers may insist the issuers to provide entire gamut of audited results upto the date of filing of the prospectus which are mentioned in the prospectus. It is also suggested that SEBI may make necessary provision to disclose the entire audited results in the prospectus.
8. The Public Sector Merchant-banker may utilise the services of brokers, sub-brokers and underwriters network more effectively for the success of the issue.

Post-Issue Management

1. In the computer era, it is quite possible to reconcile the accounts of collecting bankers quickly by the controlling bank. But, the collecting bankers or banker to issue make delay to reconcile the accounts purposefully and thereby wants to keep the funds for some time. It is suggested that SEBI may direct the bankers not to keep the funds for long time and instruct them to reconcile the accounts within certain number of days after the closing of issue.
2. The Registrar to the Issue may invest additional funds to increase the infrastructure facilities. Further, the SEBI may inspect the infrastructure requirements for the Registrar to the Issue and check up the infrastructure facilities at the time of the renewal of the registration with the SEBI.
3. The number of listing may be based on the issue size.
4. SEBI may insist on a daily collection list from the bankers to the issue. Such a list would help to finalise the closing date of the issue and expedite the allotment.
5. The stipulation of minimum 5 shareholders for one lakh rupees for the listing in the stock exchange may be removed.

SEBI and Stock Exchanges

1. The merchant-bankers are responsible for the dud issue. Therefore, it is suggested to form an expert committee or legal cell within the organisation to

select the viable project and not to handle the unviable projects.

2. SEBI may reconsider the three years track record of dividend payment stipulation for the issuer who enters into the primary market. It is suggested that it may be relaxed, taking into consideration of sluggish primary market and strict norms for availing bank loan by the issuer.
3. The stock exchange authorities may consider the ever increasing cost of advertisement, printing and postage charges and enhance the non-mandatory cost percentage in public issue expenditure.
4. SEBI may reconsider non-mandatory underwriting. It is recommended that mandatory underwriting may again be introduced to safeguard the devolvement of the issue.
5. SEBI may intimate the expiry time or the renewal time to the merchant-bankers. This will reduce the default of remittance of the renewal fees.
6. At the time of re-registration or renewal, the SEBI may examine the track record of the merchant-banker in respect of issues handled by them.
7. It is highly difficult to share and fix up the responsibility with multiple lead managers. It is also difficult to co-ordinate them and this leads to confusion. Therefore, it is suggested that SEBI may remove the requirements of multiple merchant-bankers based on issue size.

New Issue Performance

1. The percentage in proportional allotment system may be better devised in such way that it enables small investors to participate more.
2. The free pricing of issues has proved that the investors have suffered losses. Therefore, it is suggested that either free pricing be abolished or the pricing formula based on an average market price

of 52 weeks similar to private placement may be followed.

3. To avoid the evils of undated shares and delisting of shares by the stock exchanges, it is recommended that the stock exchange authorities may restrict the number of listings.
4. In free pricing era, there is a possibility of receiving the dud issues from the issuer, but the lead merchant-bankers may be selective in new issue flotation. For this purpose, the lead merchant-banker may have their own assessment; net work of critical appraisal of projects. All the merchant-bankers may be permitted to appraise the projects by SEBI.
5. Most of the projects are financed entirely by equity without recourse of debt. Therefore, SEBI may prescribe a debt equity ratio for the new issues. This will indirectly prompt the debt market.
6. The merchant-bankers may be rated by authorised rating agencies based on post listing prices of securities handled by the merchant-bankers among other factors.

General Suggestions for the Development of New Issue Management

1. The merchant-bankers may pay much attention to the equity and industry Analysis research. This will invariably help to speed up the due diligence, project appraisal, pricing the issues etc.
2. It is suggested that the Association of Merchant-bankers may take necessary steps in collaboration with Universities and Institutions in the Capital Market to train the existing as well as new merchant-bankers. Further, the Association may disseminate necessary information to prospective investors to have more and more knowledge about the New Issue Management.
3. The merchant-bankers may make a representation to the institution which are conducting training

courses and to reduce the course fees for the training so that more merchant-bankers may participate in the training courses.

4. The merchant-bankers may request to the SEBI to conduct the special training courses with reasonable fees for the merchant-bankers yearly once at major capital centres of the Country.
5. At present, the employees strength of the private merchant-bankers is not sufficient and their salaries are not in accordance with existing scales of pay of the public sector merchant-bankers. Therefore, it is suggested that the private merchant-bankers may enhance the existing scales of pay for their staff so as to develop human resources.
6. As such there is no direct relationship between the public investors and merchant-bankers, many public investors were not aware of the role of the merchant-bankers in the new issue management. Therefore, it is suggested that the merchant-bankers have to develop a large public investors base and cultivate the equity culture in their minds by way of conducting investor's conferences and releasing journals through merchant-bankers association. It would be helpful to approach the public investor directly and would also help to promote new issue business.
7. The merchant-bankers are responsible for making the market for the scrips that they have introduced. Therefore, the SEBI has to make necessary arrangements to introduce market making in new issues by the merchant-bankers so that it will enable them to develop the new issue.
8. It is suggested that the public issue cost can be reduced by using list of addresses of rejected applicants of the issuer who have already made public issue.
9. There are merchant-bankers who even go to the extent of inflating the project cost just to satisfy some stock exchange listing requirements or SEBI

guidelines. Hence, it is suggested that a strict implementation of the existing guidelines. In this regard, SEBI may set up agency to monitor the implementation of the project undertaken by the issuer.

10. It is recommended that the lead merchant-banker may invest a minimum 10 per cent of share capital that he manages. It is then only possible to prevent the merchant-banker to take up more number of assignments simultaneously.

11. The merchant-banker may disclose in each prospectus, the key details of all the past issues managed by them, including offer prices and current market prices of thc issues.

12. The SEBI may reconsider the monitoring limit of both merchant-bankers and Financial Institutions and it may be reduced to Rs. 50 crore from Rs. 500 crore. Further, the SEBI may also make it compulsory on the part of the merchant-bankers to monitor the trading behaviour of shares and its price and listing requirements etc. These measures will definitely improve the primary market and gives some status to the merchant bankers.

13. It is recommended that the SEBI may obtain information regarding the status of the project and fund utilisation from each issuer periodically.

14. Another suggestion to the SEBI is that the issuer may not be allowed to utilise the allotment and calls money without any development of the project. It is also suggested that SEBI may reconsider the stipulation that capital issue shall be fully paid up within a year in respect of issues below Rs. 500 crore.

15. SEBI has the power to examine the premises of intermediaries like merchant-bankers and registrars. But the problem lies mostly with the issuing companies, which are not under the control of SEBI. Therefore, it is recommended that the Ministry of Finance may formulate a comprehensive regulation

on security market especially in the new issue market and grant more powers to SEBI in this regard.

16. SEBI and Stock Exchange may raise the public offer component in initial public offer from the existing 25 per cent to 40 per cent.

17. At present, an entrance test for the intermediaries is optional, but it may be made compulsory. This will improve the performance of the intermediaries qualitatively.

Bibliography

Books

1. Ashoka Guha, (Ed.) (1990). *Economic Liberalisation, Industrial Structure and Growth in India.* Bombay: Oxford University Trust.
2. Avadhani, V.A., (1996), *Investment Management.* Bombay: Himalaya Publishing House.
3. Bhalla, U.K., (1983), *Investment Management, Security Analysis and Portfolio Management,* New Delhi: S Chand.
4. Bhatia, B., (1976), *New Issue Market of India.* Bombay: Vora and Company Publishers.
5. Chempen, Stanley, (1984), *The Rise of Merchant Banking.* London: George Allen And Unwin.
6. Cohen L.R.L., Clay, and Whables, (1984), *Modern Merchant Banking.* London: Woodhead and Fackerer.
7. Derrick, G. Hanson (1985), *Dictionary of Banking and Finance.* Great Britain: Pitman Publishing Ltd.
8. Deshmukh, C.D., (Ed.) 1972), *Economic and Social Development.* (1st edn.), Bombay: Vora and Company Publishers Private Ltd.
9. Dhankar, J.N., (1986), *A Treatise On Merchant Banking—Project Approval and Financing.* (1st edn.), New Delhi: Skylark Publications.
10. Gupta, L.C., (Ed.) (1976), *Readings in Industrial Finance.* Delhi: MacMillian Company of India Ltd.
11. Gupta, L.C., (1985), *Shareholders Survey Report.* New Delhi: Management Development Institute.
12. Hart, A.E., (1983), *A Key to the Stock Exchange and Investments.* London: Blackie and Son Ltd.
13. Henderson, R.F., (1957), *The New Issue Market and the Finance of Industry,* Cambridge: Bowes and Bowes.

14. Kastur Chand Lalwani, (Ed.), (1959), *Indian Capital Market.* (1st edn.), Calcutta: Artha Vanijya Gabesana Mandir.

15. Kellett, Richard, (1967), *The Merchant Banking Arena,* (1st edn.), New York: St. Martin's Press.

16. Khan, M.Y., (1978), *New Issues Market and Finance for Industry in India.* Bombay: Allied Publishers.

17. ......(1982), *Industrial Finance.* New Delhi: Tata McGraw Hill.

18. Kuchhal, S.C., (1987), *Corporation Finance—Principles and Problems.* Allahabad: Chaitanya Publishing House.

19. Kulkarni, P.V., (1987), *Corporation Finance—Principles and Problems.* Bombay: Himalaya Publishing House.

20. Laster Robert Bittel, (Ed.) (1978), *Encyclopedia of Professional Management.* Danbury: Grolier International.

21. Manjit Singh Narang, (Ed.) (1997), *International Industries Annual 1996.* New Delhi.

22. Manson, G.P., (Ed.) (19872), *Merchant Banking Service Banking,* (2nd edn.) London: Institute of Bankers.

23. Mulky, M.A., (1948), *The New Capital Issue Market in India.* Bombay: The Popular Book Depot.

24. Nadda, N.L., (1965), *Capital Market in India.* Patna: Bharathi Bhawan.

25. Naresh Kumar Gupta, (1993), *Lease Financing Concept and Practice.* (1st edn.), New Delhi: Deep and Deep Publications.

26. Narta, S.S., (1994), *Capital Issues in India.* New Delhi: Kanishka Publishing House.

27. Patel, G.S., (1987), *Stock Exchanges in India—Emerging Scenario and Challenges.* Bombay: The A.D. Shroff Memorial Trusts.

28. Sharma, K.K., et al., (1994), *Working of Stock Exchanges in India.* Jaipur: Universal Book Publishers.

29. ....(1994), *Issues in Capital Market.* Jaipur: Management Communications.

30. Shenoy, G.V., and Madan Pant, (1994), *Statistical Methods in Business and Social Sciences.* (1st edn.), Delhi: MacMillian India Ltd.

31. Shiva Ramu, S., (1995), *Global Financial Services Industry.* Delhi: South Asia Publications.

32. Simha, S.L.N., (Ed.), (1972), *Economic and Social Development.* (1st edn.), Delhi: Vora and Company Publishers Pvt. Ltd.

33. ....(1960), *The Capital Market of India.* (1st edn.), Bombay: Vora and Company Publishers Pvt. Ltd.

34. ....(1979), *Introduction to Security Analysis.* Madras: Institute of Financial Management and Research.

35. Srivastava, R.M., (1984), *Management of Indian Financial Institutions.* Bombay: Himalaya Publishing Company.

36. Subir Kumar Banerjee, (1997), *Financial Management.* (1st edn.) New Delhi: S. Chand and Company Ltd.

37. Sur, A.K., (1961), *The New Issue Market.* Calcutta: Chatterji and Company.

38. Vinayagam, N. (Ed), (1997), *Indian Banking By 2000 AD.* Delhi: Kanishka Publishers and Distributors.

39. Zacharias Thomas, (Ed), (1998), *Current Topics in Economics Commerce and Management.* (1st edn.), New Delhi: Discovery Publishing House.

Thesis

1. Agarwal Krishna Kumar, (1997), New Issue Market Operations in India. Unpublished, University of Gorakpur.

2. Gujarati, M, (1981), Performance of New Equity Shares: An Indian Experience. Doctoral Dissertation, Indian Institute of Management, Ahemadabad.

3. Indumathi Parthasarathy, (1990), Corporate Public Issues (with special Reference to Equity Issues of Industrial Companies in South India). University of Madras.

4. Jagdish Chandra Verma, (1986), Organisation and Management of Merchant Banking in India and its impact on Capital Structure of Corporate Sector. Doctoral Dissertation, University of Delhi.

5. Manas Pandy, (1997), New Issue Market Management in India. Unpublished, Mahatma Gandhi Kashi Vidyapith, Varanasi.

6. Meenakshi Sundaram, R. (1997), Services of Merchant-bankers—A study with reference to new issue management. Doctoral Dissertation, Annamalai University.

Manuals

1. *Capital Issues (Control) Act Manual.* (1983), New Delhi: The Institute of Company Secretaries of India.

2. *Compendium of Primary Market Intermediaries, Mutual Funds and Foreign Institutional Investors,* (1995), Bombay: Securities and Exchange Board of India.

3. *National Stock Exchange Info Banks* (1994), Bombay: Dalal Street Communication Ltd.
4. *Manual of SEBI Guidelines,* (1994), (4th edn.), New Delhi: Nabhi Publication.
5. *Securities Contracts (Regulation) Act 1956 Manual.* (1983), New Delhi: The Institute of Company Secretaries of India.

Journals

1. Agarwal, N. C., (1980), "Underwriting Operations in India: Re-examination Needed". *Chartered Accountant,* Vol. 28, No. 11, May pp. 1001–1005,
2. AMBI, (1996), "A concept note on Book Building process in Indian Public Issues," *Stock Exchange Review,* 20th April-19th May, pp. 14-19.
3. Anjali Shah, (1997), "Of Broken Promises and shattered dreams", *Express Investment Week,* 30 Dec. 30-5th Jan., pp. 18-21.
4. Anshuman, A.S., and Prakash Chandra, R, (1991), "Small Equity Shareholdings: The Repurcussions", *Chartered Secretary,* Vol. 21, No 7, July, pp. 562-567.
5. Anup Kumar Chaugh, (1993), "Underwriting of Public Issues", *State Bank of India Monthly Review,* Vol. XXXII No. 2, Feb., pp. 67-74.
6. Balachander, S, (1995), "Merchant-bankers: singled out—for collective errors", *The Economic Times,* 7th Dec., p. 17.
7. Batra G.S., (1996), "Merchant Banking in India: Emerging Trends in the Capital Market", *XLRI Jamshedpur Management and Labour Studies,* Vol. 21, No.1, Jan., pp. 33-41.
8. ...., and Narinder Kaur, (1995), "Financial Services in India: Emerging Trends", *South Asian Journal of Management,* Vol. 2, No. 2 April-June, pp. 33-42.
9. Bhatt, M.C., (1980), "Merchant Banking in India: Its Contribution to National Development", *Chartered Secretary,* Vol. 10, No. 10, October, p. 922.
10. Bhatt R. S., (1992), "Genesis and Development of Capital Market in India", *The Journal of the Indian Institute of Bankers,* Vol. 63 No. 2, March, pp. 16-25.
11. Bhole L.M., (1995), "The Indian Capital Market at Cross Roads", *Vikalpa* Vol. 20, No. 2, April-June, pp. 29-41.

12. Bombay Bureau, (1995), "Merchant-bankers, Others Welcome Suggestions", *The Economic Times,* 13 July, p. 7.

13. Calcutta Bureau, (1996), "Sidbi plans refinance for market-marking in new issues" *The Economic Times,* 25 Feb., p. 1.

14. Chandra Prasanna, (1991), "Indian Capital Market : Pathways of Development", *Chartered Financial Analyst,* Vol. 5, No. 4, Jan.-Feb., pp. 3-9.

15. Chandrasekhar Krishnamurti, (1995), "Contractual forms and the process of going public in select countries", *The ICFAI Journal of Applied Finance* Vol. I, No. 2, July, pp. 84-89.

16. Dhagat D.K., (1992), "Pricing of Issues", *State Bank of India Monthly Review,* Vol. XXXXI, Nov, pp. 38-48.

17. Fermando V.S., (1995), "Performance Survey of Merchant Bankers", *Quarterly Money Manager, Business Standard,* Aug.-Oct., pp. 70-81.

18. ...., (1995), "Rosy Projections, Poor Performances Make Prospectuses Meaningless," *The Merchant Banker Update,* Sep., pp. 25-43.

19. ...., (1995), "Preferential Allottees are the Biggest Loser", *The Merchant Banker Update.* Aug., pp. 18-24.

20. ...., (1995), "Who to Blame? Free pricing has proved costly for investors", *The Merchant Banker Update,* July, pp. 15-22.

21. ...., (1995), "Half-yearly Rankings", *The Merchant Banker Update,* December, pp. 28-59.

22. Financial Response Feature, (1994), "Merchant Banking Services in North India", *The Economic Times,* New Delhi, 28th April, pp. I-VIII.

23. Ghani A. H., (1996), "The Indian Capital Market where is the level playing field?", *The Merchant Banker Update,* July, pp. 30-32.

24. Indrajit Basu, (1995), "Retailing of a Mega Issue", *Dalal Street Journal,* 17-30, April, pp. 28-29.

25. Jain, P.K., (1979), "UTI and The New Issue Market", *Artha Vijnana,* Vol 21, No. 2. July, p. 218.

26. Jhaveri N.J., (1995), "Unsavoury reputation of Merchant-bankers," *The Merchant Banker Update,* October, pp. 28-29.

27. Kamalaksha, M., (1993), "SBI Capital Markets Ltd.—Its functions and performance", *State Bank of India Monthly Review,* Vol XXXII, No. 3, March, pp. 110-120.

28. Kamal Nayan Kabra, (1994), "India's Financial Sector: Overgrowth and Dysfunctionalities", *Productivity,* Vol. 35, No. 2, July-Sep., pp. 200-210.

29. Karthikeyan. M., (1997), "Weeding them out", *Business India,* 22nd Sep. - 5th Oct., p. 101.

30. Kensource Information Services, (1996), "Institutional Appraisals: Will they ensure quality issues?" *The Merchant Banker Update,* July, pp. 69-70.

31. Khan, M.Y., (1977), "New Issue Market and Company Finance", *Economic & Political Weekly,* Vol. 12, March, pp. M11-M21.

32. Kothari Rajesh, (1986), "Profile of Recent Developments in Indian Capital Market", *Prashanika,* HCM-RIPA, Vol. XV, No., 4, October-December, pp. 110-125.

33. Kulishreshtha C.M., (1995), "Book Building for Primary Issues", *The Merchant Banker Update.* Vol. XV, No. 4, October-December pp. 36-37.

34. Lakshmi Krishnan, (1995), "Issue Pre-writing" *Chartered Financial Analyst,* Nov, pp. 38-39.

35. Lal, T., (1990), "Primary Capital Market: Some Reflections", *Yojana,* Vol. 34, 16th-30th June, pp. 9-12.

36. Malati Anagol, (1990), "Merchant Banking: Emerging Areas in India Context", *The Journal of the Indian Institute of Bankers.* Vol. 61, No. 3, July-Sep., pp. 128-132.

37. Mantry, R.B., (1989), "Growth of Capital Market and Investing Public - Some Non-issues", *The Chartered Accountant,* Vol. 37, No. 12, June, pp. 1079-1080.

38. Mayya, M.R., (1997), "How to turn on Small Investor", *The Economic Times,* 14 June, p. 5.

39. Mohan Sule, (1990), "SEBI comes down on misleading Advertisements", *The Economic Times,* 30 Dec., p. 12.

40. Nand Dhameja, (1994), "Capital Market-Emerging Trends", *Productivity,* Vol. 35, No. 2, July-Sep., pp. 238-248.

41. Naresh Kumar, (1991), "Shareholding Pattern in India: Areas for Reform", *Chartered Secretary,* April, pp. 228-244.

42. ....(1995), "Myths of Due Diligence", *The Merchant Banker Update,* July, pp. 24-25.

43. Neeti Jain, and Rishi Roop Tripathi, (1996), "The Rules that SEBI Made", *The Economic Times,* 15 July, p.v.

44. News Bureau, (1996), "Hard-to-Hawk Public issues", *The Merchant Banker Update,* 15 July, p. 46.

45. Opinion Poll, (1995), "The State of Primary Market", *The Merchant Banker Update,* Sep., pp. 19-23.

46. Panda, J.K., (1998), "Equity Allotment. A Critical Analysis", *Journal of Accounting and Finance,* Vol. 2, No. 1, April, pp. 30-34.

47. Pandya, V.H., (1992), "Securities and Exchange Board of India, Its Role, Powers, Functions and Activities", *Chartered Secretary,* Vol. 22, No. 9, September, p. 783.

48. Paresh Mehata, (1995), "Primary Pitfalls", *Dalal Street Journal,* 15-28 May, pp. 158-159.

49. Paul Marriage, (1995), "Anatomy of an IPO" *World Executive's Digest,* Vol. XVI, No. 6, June, pp. 12-14.

50. Philip George, (1996), "A Shortage of Lawerys at SEBI", *Business World,* 7-29 Feb., pp. 122-123.

51. "Primary Market", (1996), *The Stock Exchange Review,* Bombay, July, pp. 16-18.

52. Primary Market Team, (1996), "Primary Colour", *The Economic Times,* 1 April, p. VIII.

53. Prithvi Haldea, (1993-94), "Handle with Care", *Business Standard– The Smart Investor Annual Issue,* pp. 61-62.

54. Puranik, Alok, (1992), "Role of Corporate Securities in Household Saving and Private Corporate Sector Financing during Eighties – Some Empirical Observations", *Chartered Secretary,* Vol. 22, No. 11, November, p. 991.

55. Rabindra Kumar Pati, (1995), "A Step by Step Approach", *The Chartered Accountant,* Apr, pp. 1418-1421.

56. Raghuvir Srinivasan, (1995), "The Primary Market Sweepstakes", *The Hindu Business Line,* 26 Feb., p. 4.

57. Rajiv Shirali, (1992), "Companies Fear Rise in Issue Costs" *The Economic Times,* 12 Jan., p. 9.

58. Rajiv Thakur, (1995), "Developments and their aftermath", *The Merchant Banker Update,* July, pp. 24-25.

59. Ram Mohan, T.T., (1980), "Equity Issues by New Unit– Patterns of Public Response", *Economic & Political Weekly,* Vol. 15, November, pp. M151-M156.

60. "Ranking of Merchant Bankers 1995-96", (1996), *The Merchant Banker Update,* July, pp. 44-61.

61. Ravishankar, T. V., (1996), "Merchant Bankers Clash Over Advisory Role" *The Economic Times,* 13, Feb., p. 4.

62. "Reliability of Profit Forecasts in Public Issue Prospectus", (1996), *The Merchant Banker Update* Feb., pp. 44-46.

63. "Report on Primary Market Reforms", (1995), *Business Today,* May 22-6 June, pp. 93-97.

64. Research Bureau, (1995), "Shaky Investors Confidence", *The Economic Time, Data Bank,* pp. 30-32.

65. *Reserve Bank of India,* (1996), "Capital Issues and Public Responses during 1991-92", Vol. I, No. 7, July, pp. 349-377.

66. *Reserve Bank of India,* (1995), "Capital Issues and Public Responses during 1986-87", Vol. XLIX, No. 2, Feb., 129-178.

67. Rose Mary, A., (1995), "The Money Class", *Financial Express,* 11 Nov., p. 1.

68. Roshmi Jayakar, (1993), "Master of the Monday Game" *Business Today,* Oct 22-6 Nov., pp. 90-94.

69. "Round Table Discussion", (1996), *The Merchant Banker Update,* Dec., pp. 16-27.

70. "Round Table Discussion', (1996), *The Merchant Banker Update,* May, pp. 16-22.

71. Saha, A., (1988), "Merchant Banking: Retrospect & Prospects", *Yojana,* Vol. XVII, No. 1. June, pp. 61-70.

72. Sankarsubramanian, K., (1996), "Merchant Bankers, increased responsibilities in new issues", *The Hindu,* June 16, p. 25.

73. Sampath Kumar, D, (1995) "Of intermediaries and facilitators", *The Hindu Business Line,* 26 March, p. 4.

74. Sarah Abraham, (1997), "Services: The Quiet revolution", *Business India,* Aug. 25- Sep. 7, pp. 66-71.

75. Senior Correspondent, (1997), "SEBI Scrap Merchant Banking Categories", *The Hindu Business Line,* Sep. 7, p. 5.

76. Shah, K. J., (1981), "Small Shareholding", *The Chartered Accountant,* Vol. 30, No. 5, November, p. 316.

77. Srinivastava, R. M., (1991), "Merchant Banking in India—A Bright Future", *Yojana,* 15 May, pp. 12-16.

78. Sucheta Dalal, (1991), "Bankers Find SEBI means Business" *The Economic Times,* 30 June, p. 10.

79. "The Merchant Banker Update-Marg Opinion poll", (1996), *The Merchant Banker Update,* June, pp. 11-24.

80. "The Primary Capital Market" (1995), *Centre for Monitoring Indian Economy,* Oct., pp. 7-47.

81. Thiripal Raju, M., (1996), "New Strategies for Making Public Issues", *The Merchant Banker Update,* June, pp. 52-54.

82. ....(1995), "EPS/P/R Ratio Abused by Merchant Bankers and Companies", *The Merchant Banker Update,* August, pp. 52-54.

83. Trikha, Kapil, (1989), "Merchant Bankers and Public Issues", *Chartered Accountant,* Vol. 38, No. 6, December, p. 477.

84. Usha Ravi, N., Sriram and Niranjan Rajadhyaksha, (1998), "Whirlwind", *Business World,* 7 Jan., pp. 30-35.

85. Vijayashanker, Na, (1992), "SEBI Guidelines : An invitation to innovation", *The Economic Times,* 1, Aug., p. I

86. Virdi B.D., and Sudhakar Shukla, (1993), "Cost and Structure of New Capital Issues", *Company News and Notes,* Vol. XXXI, No. 3, Sep., pp. 3-8.

87. Viswanathan, M., (1995), "Indian Merchant Banking: Coping with Change" *The Merchant Banker Update,* 1 July, pp. 27-32.

Reports

1. Association of Merchant Bankers in India, (1996), "Concept note on Book Building process in Indian Public issues", Special Report, Bombay: *The Stock Exchange Review,* 20th April-19 May.

2. Malegam, Y.H. (1994), "Recommendation of the Melegam Committee Report". Bombay: *Securities and Exchange Board of India.*

3. Government of India, "Annual Report on the working and administration of companies", *Department of Company Affairs*–Various Issues.

4. Investment Week, (1997), "New Issue Flash Back", Madras: *The Financial Express.* 5th Jan.-29th June.

5. Patel G.S. (1986), "Report of High Power Committee (Patel) on working of stock exchanges in India", New Delhi: *Ministry of Finance.*

6. Rengarajan C, (1982), "Study Group on Financing of the Private Corporate Sector in the Sixth Five Year Plan", New Delhi: *Planning Commission,* Government of India.

7. Reserve Bank of India, (1991), "A Report of Committee on Financial System", Bombay: *RBI,* November.

8. Singh, D.R., et al., (1993), "Management of Public Issues—Role of Merchant Bankers and Company Management", (Working Paper) Ludhiana: Department of Business Management, *Punjab Agricultural University.*

Other Publication

1. "Capital Market during Eighties", Bombay: *Securities and Exchange Board of India.*
2. "Company News and Notes", New Delhi: *Government of India,* Department of Company Affairs—Various issues.
3. "Controller of Capital Issues", New Delhi: *Government of India,* Various Issues.
4. "Economic Survey", 1996-97, 1997-98, New Delhi: *Government of India,* Ministry of Finance.
5. "News Letter", Bombay: *Securities and Exchange Board of India,* Various Issues.
6. Prime Directory", (1996-1997), New Delhi: *Praxis Consultants Private Limited.*
7. "RBI Bulletin", (1983-84 to 1989-90 and July 1994, July 1996) Bombay: *Reserve Bank of India.*
8. Report on Currency and Finance" (1992-93), Bombay: *Reserve Bank of India.*
9. "Stock Exchange Official Directory", Bombay: *Bombay Stock Exchange,* Various Issues.
10. "The Stock Market Today", Bombay: *Bombay Stock Exchange,* Various issues.

ANNEXURE I

Pattern of Investment, Savings and Capital Inflow (% of GDP)

Plan Period	*GDI*	*GDS*	*CAB*
I	10.8	10.4	0.4
II	15.3	12.4	2.9
III	16.7	14.3	2.4
IV	17.2	14.9	2.3
V	17.8	17.0	0.8
VI	21.6	21.9	–0.3
VII	23.8	22.4	1.5

Note: GDI–Gross Domestic Investment, GDS–Gross Domestic Savings CAB–Current Account Balance, GDP–Gross Domestic Product.

Sources: Central Statistical Organisation, National Income Accounts quoted in Economic Liberalisation, Industrial Structure and Growth in India, edited by Ashoka Guha, Oxford University Press 1990, p. 138.

ANNEXURE II

Proportionate share of different financial assets in the financial savings of the household sector in India

Year	*Deposit in Banking and Non–Banking*	*LIC, PFS and Pension funds*	*Share and debentures of companies*	*Units of UTI*	*Others**
1980-81	48.9	25.1	3.4	0.3	22.3
1985-86	47.1	23.4	5.5	2.3	21.7
1986-87	50.3	22.7	5.6	3.0	18.4
1987-88	44.3	25.2	2.3	3.3	24.9
1988-89	40.4	27.2	3.9	3.5	25.0
1989-90	38.0	26.0	6.4	4.1	25.5
1990-91	32.2	29.2	8.7	6.0	23.9
1991-92	31.1	28.9	6.1	14.9	19.0
1992-93	38.9	29.8	10.3	6.4	14.6
1993-94	36.8	29.0	10.3	6.0	17.9

* Others include holdings in currency and claims on Government.

Source: Report on Currency and Finance, Reserve Bank of India, 1992–93. *Reserve Bank of India Monthly Collection,* July 1994.

ANNEXURE III

Indian Corporate Sector Performance and New Issue of Public Limited Companies

(Rs. in crore)

Year	*Industrial Growth Rate (%)*	*New Issues (Equity) of Public Limited Companies*
1983-84	5.5	382
1984-85	5.6	383
1985-86	8.7	858
1986-87	9.1	1008
1987-88	7.3	1103
1988-89	8.7	1103
1989-90	8.3	1129

Source: Reserve Bank of India Bulletin–Various Issues.

ANNEXURE IV

New Issues by Non-Government Public Limited Companies

(Rs. in crores)

Year	*Equity*	*Preference*	*Debentures*	*Total*
1975	50	5	3	58
1980	89	2	73	164
1981	280	2	196	478
1982	259	2	445	706
1983-84	382	2	454	838
1984-85	383	–	693	1056
1985-86	858	1	843	1702
1986-87	1008	0.7	1556	2565
1987-88	1103	6.8	667	1777
1988-89	1033	3.3	2188	3225
1989-90	1219	7.9	5246	6473
1990-91	1284	13.1	3015	4312
1991-92	1731	1.5	4024	5756
1992-93	9961	0.5	9844	19826
1993-94	10113	63.5	9325	19501
1994-95	17454	131.3	8871	26456

Source: Report on Currency and Finance, Reserve Bank of India, various issues quoted by L.M. Bhole in his study on "The Indian Capital Market at Crossroads", *Vikalpa,* Vol. 20, No. 2, April–June, 1995. p. 38.

ANNEXURE V

Growth of Capital Market

Item	*1980*	*1992*	*1994*	*1996*
Market Capitalisation (Rs. in crores)	5843	275000	398432	519000
No. of Stock Exchanges	8	21	23	23
No. of listed Companies	2265	6500	6800	7500
No. of Shareholders (In Millions)	2	15	16	20
'No. of New Issues	–	512	1154	1428
Total Amount Raised through Rights and Public (Rs. in crores)	–	5562.6	21850.2	10981.7

Source: Compiled from The Hindu Survey of Indian Industry 1993, *Vikalpa* Vol. 20, No. 2, April–June, 1995 p. 38, and Prime Data Base, Stock Exchange Review May, 1996, and The Chartered Accountant, Nov. 1996, p. 42 and Business India, Aug, 14–27, 1995, pp. 62–71.

ANNEXURE VI

Consents and Acknowledgement Granted by the CCI and SEBI

Year	*Capital Issue Raised*	*Bonus Issue Raised*	*Total*
1961	132.70	5.81	138.51
1962	163.04	11.40	174.44
1963	141.47	11.12	152.59
1964	138.95	2.33	141.28
1965	86.27	15.66	101.93
1966	66.03	73.40	139.43
1967	150.67	70.44	221.11
1968	87.43	22.84	110.27
1969	86.44	22.00	108.44
1970	49.03	44.28	93.31
1971	85.16	26.87	112.03
1972	112.45	34.94	147.39

(Contd...)

Year	*Capital Issue Raised*	*Bonus Issue Raised*	*Total*
1973	110.71	41.97	152.48
1974	103.61	74.90	178.51
1975	156.88	72.84	229.72
1976	139.78	90.37	230.51
1977	190.05	125.59	315.64
1978	160.31	90.28	250.59
1979	269.67	83.15	352.82
1980	338.80	125.40	464.20
1981	526.57	101.80	628.37
1982	774.10	150.50	924.60
1983	858.60	82.50	941.10
1984-85	1699.10	88.30	1787.40
1985-86	2931.30	235.50	3166.80
1986-87	4213.90	302.60	4516.50
1987-88	2163.00	296.00	3459.00
1988-89	4932.00	196.00	5128.00
1989-90	7567.00	352.00	7919.00
1990-91	6122.50	300.70	6423.20
1991-92	11989.00	352.50	12341.40
1992-93	20794.00	—	20794.00*
1993-94	17121.00	—	17121.00*

* Exclude Bonus share in 1992–93 and 1993–94. From 1961–1983 refers to January–December. From 1984–85 to 1993–94 refers to April–March.

Source: Controller of Capital Issues, Ministry of Finance, Government of India and Securities and Exchange Board of India.

ANNEXURE VII

Public Issue Scenario in India

Year	*No. of Issues*	*Amount Raised*	*No. of Merchant-bankers*	*No. of Lead MBs*
1987-88	122	1627.97	N.A.	—
1988-89	150	1291.74	N.A.	N.A.
1989-90	187	2793.26	78	36
1990-91	141	1704.36	82	71
1991-92	196	1711.36	312	80
1992-93	528	6060.83	324	130
1993-94	770	12344.04	475	240
1994-95	1343	13111.60	816	349
1995-96	1428	11822.00	1151	400
1996-97	753	11648.00	1163	N.A.
1997-98	62	2861.94	300	N.A.

N.A. Refers to Not available

Source: Compiled from Prime Database quoted by *Business India,* November 17–30, 1997, p. 29 and *The Hindu* 23, November, 1998, p. 12.

ANNEXURE VIII

Merchant Banking Milestones

1967	A concept arrives-India's first merchant banking division set up by the Grindlays Bank.
1970	End of monopoly—First National City Bank setup merchant banking division.
1972	Nationalised Banks entered into fray as per the Banking Commission recommendations.
1973	Development Banks (ICICI) and Share Broking Firms (FICOM) joined Merchant Banking Bandwagon.
1980	Boom in the Stock Market Entry on large number of brokers firms and banks.
1984.	Commercial Banks permitted to start the leasing and financial services subsidiaries.
1988	Formation of SEBI on 12th April 1988.
1990	Government of India brought out first guidelines for Merchant Bankers. Creation of three categories of Merchant Bankers by SEBI.
1992	Controller of Capital Issues Abolished. Primary market rush begins in free pricing era. Enactment of Merchant Bankers Regulations and Rules by SEBI.
1993	Smaller Merchant Bankers return to market.
1994	Threat of severe competition.
1995	Big Lead Merchant Banker SBI Capital Markets Limited under shadow of investigation.
1996	Entry norms for issuers revised. Inspection of top 30 Merchant Bankers.
1997	Debars 64 Merchant Bankers who have not furnished employees information. Scraping of 3 different categories of merchant-bankers and ban on fund-based services.

ANNEXURE IX

Location of Sampled Merchant-bankers Zone-wise and Institutions-wise

Zone	*Merchant-banker Group*						*Total*
	AFI	*SFI*	*NB*	*NBS*	*PSB*	*PMB*	
West:							
Mumbai	–	–	1	–	–	5	6
North:							
New Delhi	1	–	–	–	–	1	2
Lucknow	–	1	–	–	–	–	1
South:							
Chennai	–	–	–	1	1	7	9
Hyderabad	–	–	1	–	–	5	6
Cochin	–	–	–	–	1	–	1
East:							
Calcutta	–	–	–	–	–	1	1
Total	1	1	2	1	2	19	26

Source: Primary Data

ANNEXURE X

List of Sample Merchant-bankers

S. No	Name of the Merchant Banker
1.	Industrial Finance Corporation of India Limited
2.	Pradeshiya Industrial and Investment Corporation of Uttar Pradesh Limited (PICUP)
3.	Corporation Bank
4.	State Bank of Hyderabad
5.	Indbank Merchant Banking Services Limited
6.	City Union Bank Limited
7.	The Federal Bank Limited
8.	Cholamandalam Investment and Finance Company Limited
9.	Prudential Capital Market Limited
10.	Dugar Finance India Limited
11.	Doogar and Associates Limited
12.	Nucleus Securities Limited
13.	Karvy Financial Services Limited
14.	Merbanc Financial Services Limited
15.	Spring Field Financial Services Limited
16.	Vijay Growth Financial Services Limited
17.	21st Century Management Services Limited
18.	India Securities Limited
19.	LKP Merchant Financing Limited
20.	S.M. Finance Limited
21.	Integrated Finance Company Limited
22.	MCC Financial Services Limited
23.	South Asian Financial Exchange Limited
24.	Wipro Financial Services Limited
25.	Khandelwal Jain Management Consultant and Financial Services Limited.
26.	Munoth Investment Limited.

ANNEXURE—XI

Statement Showing the Lead Merchant Bankers, Issuers Name, Issue Price and Market Price

Sl. No.	*Issuers Name*	*Lead Merchant Bankers Name*	*Issue Price*	*Market Price*
1	*2*	*3*	*4*	*5*
1.	Welcome Coir Industries	Prudential Capital Markets Ltd. Rusoday and Company	15.00	09.10
2.	Modern Home Credit Capital Ltd.	Prudential Capital Markets Ltd.	30.00	20.00
3.	Freedom Industries Ltd.	Indbank Merchant Banking Services	15.00	16.40
4.	Swetha Engineering Limited	Indbank Merchant Banking Services/21st Century Finance and Management	20.00	9.10
5.	Chetak Spintex Limited	Indbank Merchant Banking Services HSIDC	12.50	10.50
6.	Ranjan Polysters Limited	Doogar and Associates	20.00	23.00
7.	Sterling Holiday Financial Services	MCC/State Bank of Travancore	15.00	7.50
8.	Kirti Seeds Biotech Limited	Prudential Capital Markets Ltd./NCL Research	21.00	N.T.
9.	Keswani Synthetics Industries	IFCI/ITC Classic	55.00	21.50
10.	Mangal Finance Limited	Prudential Capital Market Ltd./Haryana Financial	30.00	5.75

(Contd.)

(Contd.)

1	2	3	4	5
11.	Majestic Industries Limited	Prudential Capital Market Ltd./Keynote Corporate Services	60.00	14.00
12.	Gupta Carpets International	Doogar and Associates	17.00	4.75
13.	Ghanshyam Steel Works Limited	Nucleus Securities/BOI Finance	12.50	27.50
14.	Shell Securities Limited	Prudential Capital Markets Ltd.	20.00	19.60
15.	Kothari Polymers Limited	India Securities	35.00	16.25
16.	Arvind Remedies Limited	Munoth Investment/PNB Capital	30.00	18.00
17.	Global Syntex (Bhilwara) Ltd.	Doogar and Associates/Aryaman Financial Services	11.00	12.00
18.	Magicut Tools Limited	Prudential Capital Markets Ltd.	17.00	12.10
19.	Shivom Granites Limited	Prudential Capital Market Ltd./Bank of Baroda	15.00	N.T
20.	Sunrice Securities Limited	Prudential Capital Market Ltd./PNB Capital/Keynote Corporate	35.00	11.00

(Annexure Contd...)

(Contd.)

1	2	3	4	5
21.	Pals Distilleries Limited	Indbank Merchant Banking Services Sudaram Finance	25.00	27.00
22.	Khemka Containers Limited	Indbank Merchant Bankaing Services/Pioneer Investment Corporation	36.00	N.T.
23.	Chandha Papers Limited	PICUP/CRB Capital Markets Ltd.	30.00	18.65
24.	Alliance Credit and Investment	Prudential Capital Markets Ltd./SBI Capital Markets Limited	100.00	10.00
25.	SRG Finance and Management Consultants	Doogar and Associates/Apple Industries	20.00	30.00
26.	SAM Industries Limited	State Bank of Hyderabad/State Bank of Travancore	15.00	11.00
27.	Afrin India Limited	Doogar and Associates	15.00	15.00
28.	Jain Studious Limited	IFCI/Shriram Investments	90.00	100.00

ANNEXURE XII

Guidelines Related to the Issue of Equity Shares

Item	*New Companies Promoted by*		*Existing Private/Closely Held/Unlisted Companies*					
	Individual	*Existing Co.,*	*Without Track Record*	*With Track Record*	*Without T.R. Promoted by Existing Co., with T.R.*	*Without T.R. Seeking Disinvestment with Fresh Capital*	*With T.R. Seeking Disinvestment with Fresh Capital*	*Existing Listed Companies*
Pricing of Issues	At Par	At Premium	At Par	At Premium	At Premium	At Par	At Premium	At Par/Pre.
Track Record of Consistent Dividend Payment	Not Required	Five years	Not required	Three years	Five years	Not required	Three years	Not required
Promoters contribution	20% Issue size	50% of issue size	20% issue size	20% of issue size	50% of issue size	20% issue size	20% issue size	20% issue size
Lock in period	3 years	3 years	3 years	3 years	3 years	3 years	3 years	3 years
Minimum subscription	Rs. 50,000	Rs. 50,000	Rs. 1,00,000	Rs. 1,00,000	Rs. 1,00,000	Rs. 1,00,000	Rs. 1,00,000	Rs. 1,00,000

Note: T.R. refers to Track Record

Source: SEBI manual

ANNEXURE XIII

Firm Allotment and Reservation in Public Issues

Name of the Institutions	*Maximum permissible allotment*
Indian and Multilateral Developmental Financial Institutions	20% of the issue
Indian Mutual funds	20% of the issue
Foreign Institutional investors (including non-resident Indians and overseas corporate bodies)	24% of the issue
Permanent employees/share-holders of the promoting companies	10% of the issue

Source: SEBI Manual.

ANNEXURE XIV

High Cost of Funds

Average cost of share issue by existing and new companies

Years	Cost of Funds
1959–66	5.00
1967–71	4.50
1972–73	6.00
1974–80	6.66–7.47
1981–85	8.20–11.50
1986–96	15.00–20.00

Note: Cost of capital issues is shown as percentage of total amount issued.

Source: *The Economic Times,* 5th September 1997, p. 9.

Index

N

O

P

R

S

T

U

V

W